Winning Together

A Parable of the Power of
Collaboration in Business

Matthias Miller

Winning Together

A Parable of the Power of Collaboration in Business

Matthias Miller

ISBN 978-1-7327783-1-3

This book is dedicated to my wife Bonita. You've taught me more about "Winning Together" than anyone else.

Thank you for supporting me, loving me, cheering me on, and never telling me "I told you so!" even if you had many rightful opportunities to do so!

Contents

Claim Your Free Bonus Resources! 1

Preface 3

Characters 5

Prologue: Into the Woods 7

Chapter 1: Warning Lights 11

Chapter 2: Welcome to Camaraderie 25

Chapter 3: You're Worth the Investment 37

Chapter 4: Win With Fewer Hours 51

Chapter 5: You're Not Alone 69

Chapter 6: "If I Don't Take Responsibility, Nobody Will" 81

Chapter 7: Unmasking the Facade 95

CONTENTS

Chapter 8: Not Just Shooting the Breeze 109

Epilogue 117

Acknowledgments 119

Claim Your Free Bonus Resources!

Your purchase of this book includes bonus resources to help you grow your business.

The *Risk Free Delegation* **video training** (along with the accompanying training guide) will give you insight on how you can hand off important parts of your business without risking customers, profit, or growth.

The *I Refuse to Be Busy* **e-book** will give you practical tools to increase your effectiveness. It is a contrarian guide to getting more done without selling your soul.

The "**Gold Rush Millionaire**" **video training** will help you understand which opportunities to pursue and why many people remain blind to the opportunities directly in front of them.

And there's more!

Visit www.winningtogetherbook.com to get your bonuses now!

Preface

I stumbled blindly into entrepreneurship.

When I first started, I was simply looking to answer a deep craving inside of me. I had no idea the answer to that craving was entrepreneurship.

Frustrated by my lack of results in business, I started studying the habits of the people who were successful. I learned they intentionally surrounded themselves with people who could help them better themselves and grow.

In my journey, I've discovered we must be very intentional about who we allow to influence us. The right people will give us a tremendous amount of energy and forward momentum, while the wrong people will knock the wind out of us.

When I started my journey, I had no idea about the vast number of well-intentioned but deeply misinformed coaches and trainers in the business arena. I've watched individual entrepreneurs slowly self-destruct because they've started ingesting toxic advice.

Discernment always comes at a price. For some, it costs a few thousand dollars. For others, it may cost tens of thousands of dollars. Unfortunately, for far too many, it ends up costing their marriage, their family, and even their health.

Discernment is simple but not easy.

If you want to know whose advice to listen to, observe their life. If you learn from them, you will become like them. And if you want to know who they are becoming, look at the lives of their mentors and the people they're learning from. Over time, that's who you will become as well.

Placing yourself into a Winning Circle with like-minded entrepreneurs will amplify the impact you can have. A group that resonates with who you are and what you want to achieve will be worth every cent of your investment, of both your time and money.

As you read this book, allow it to challenge you to become more intentional in building powerful relationships in business. I urge you to find the people you can run with in this season of life and go for it!

Let's win together.

 Matthias

Characters

MAIN CHARACTERS

- **Jack Martin** - Mechanic
- **Cal** - Jack's Mentor

CAL'S WINNING CIRCLE

- **Carl** - Pilot
- **Trevor Young** - Educator
- **Kip** - Restaurateur
- **Charlie** - Rancher

OTHER CHARACTERS

- **Riley Martin** - Jack's wife
- **Pete, Nate, and Gabriel** - Jack's Employees

Prologue: Into the Woods

"WHEN IS Daddy gonna be home, Momma?"

The woman winced and turned away from the window. She had thought long and hard about this moment, but still found herself stumbling over what to say to her little boy. Her pulse quickened and her stomach churned. She wished she could ignore the question. She didn't want to face the reality she couldn't explain.

She knew one thing-she wouldn't lie to him.

"I don't know, Jack. I don't know if he'll ever come back."

"But Mr. Barkley will find him, won't he?"

"Sheriff Barkley and all his deputies have done everything they can, dear." A tear rolled down her cheek and she pulled her six-year-old close. "All we can do is pray he'll come back."

She held the boy tightly for a few minutes before going into the kitchen to begin making supper.

Jack watched his momma walk away, a heavy feeling growing in the pit of his stomach. He grabbed his raincoat and boots and slipped out onto the porch where Muffin, his Irish-red cocker-spaniel eagerly waited for him. He looked

into the garage, wishing he could watch his dad tinker
with cars again like he always did after work. Jack didn't
understand what he felt in his chest and stomach, but he
didn't like it.

He made his way down the muddy driveway, hopping in
and out of the puddles. He was getting soaked from head
to foot. He came to the end of the driveway and gazed
longingly at the muddy field across the street. The rain
from earlier in the morning had turned the field into a
gigantic muddy slip-and-slide. He looked at Muffin and
motioned toward the street.

"We can't go over there. Momma won't let us." He sat on
the muddy gravel as the dog nuzzled him, as if to comfort
him. Suddenly, he perked up. "We could go play in the
woods," he said to the dog. "Yeah! Let's go into the woods
and build a fort!" he repeated, getting excited.

Sensing his excitement the dog stood up and barked in
agreement.

"Come-on girl!" He shouted and ran off to the woods,
Muffin bounding ahead of him. Suddenly she spotted a
squirrel and darted off among the trees. Jack ran to keep
up with her, scrambling over branches and through leaves.
Jack called for the dog to stop, yelling above her insistent
barking. She kept running, so he stumbled on. Exhausted,
he finally caught up to her.

"Muffin," he scolded, "you shouldn't have run so far! We
need to get home for supper."

He turned to head home. The well worn footpath was nowhere in sight. Which way should he go? He turned again and began pushing through brush. Nothing seemed familiar. Confused, he ran blindly the way he thought he'd come. As he broke into a clearing, his foot slipped in the mud.

Jack slid down a creek bank as dusk crowded in.

Chapter 1: Warning Lights

Years later...

JACK MARTIN's Tacoma sputtered its way into the auto-shop parking lot. He shoved the gear into park causing the truck to grumble and die. He moaned at the sound. It was already six o'clock in the morning, later than he had hoped. He cursed the dead battery and hurried to the door, fumbling with the wad of keys at his side. He jammed one into the office knob. Wrong key. He found the right one, twisted it, and burst into the office, dust flying through the morning rays of the sun.

He plopped down at his desk and started leafing through the files before him, already compiling a to-do list in his mind.

Mrs. Taylor's Jetta needed a new catalytic converter; Rod Wilson needed an oil change and couldn't find access to the battery on his Corolla. Easy fix, those late 80's Corolla batteries are only accessible from the bottom.

Then there was all the paperwork and bills and follow-up calls on top of that...

"Don't forget about Jimmy's first tee-ball game tomorrow afternoon," his wife had reminded him the night before.

"And do you think you'll be home in time to go with me to the church banquet in the evening?"

"I don't know yet. We'll see," he had murmured before shutting off the lights.

Jack found himself staring numbly at a paper before him: It was an invitation to a "business breakfast" taking place on the following Saturday. "Share, learn, and grow with people like you!" it read. He set it aside to deal with later, knowing it would eventually make its way into the trash.

Payroll, rent, an order for supplies, and the four voicemails left on his cell during off hours.

Jack took a deep breath, tightened his lips, and dove in.

MOMENTS LATER, Pete, Jack's right-hand man, stuck his head through the office door.

"Hey boss, you got a moment?" the man asked, sitting down across the desk from Jack.

"Yeah, Pete," Jack said, looking up from his laptop, trying not to feel irritated at the interruption. "What's up?"

"Well," the young man began, shifting in his seat, "it's about time off—not that I'm asking for extra time off, necessarily, it's just..." he stuttered. Jack leaned back, trying to set his employee at ease. He figured it was the "approachable boss" thing to do.

"Well, my brother's getting married next month, and I was wondering if I could use some vacation time to take a week off for it."

Jack brought his arms up behind his head, confusing the dust still floating lazily through the morning light. He thought about how to respond.

Pete was a hardworking man, the best mechanic Jack had ever employed. They had worked together for years, and he had proven himself a diligent and hardworking employee. Surely he deserved some paid time off.

But there was so much to do. It would mean extra work for both of them leading up to Pete's time off and less production while he was away.

The business was getting by, but could they really afford even a week's loss in revenue?

"I don't know, Pete," the boss finally said, trying to sound optimistic. "That's a long time for you to be away. We are barely keeping up as it is so, without you, we'd have to cut back. I just don't know if we can afford to do that right now."

Pete watched a roach scurry under the metal desk. He furrowed his brow, thinking.

"How about Nate? He could step up for me while I'm gone," the younger mechanic suggested.

"Nate doesn't have near the experience you do. I'd end up spending all my time in the garage helping him rather than taking care of all the paperwork, follow-ups, and whatnot." Jack picked up the papers and plopped them back down to drive home his point.

"You've got to understand, Pete"—Jack searched for eye contact—"I wish I could let you go for a week, but I just can't."

Pete met his boss's eyes.

"I understand," he conceded and began to get up.

"I tell you what," Jack inserted as Pete rose to his feet. "I'll let you have a long weekend over the wedding. Send me the date and I'll write it into the calendar. But unfortunately, I can't give you a whole week's vacation."

"Thank you, sir." Pete nodded and turned to go.

"You're my man, Pete!"

The door swung shut.

JACK WATCHED as his man walked back toward the garage.

"What a way to start the day," he mumbled as he wiggled his mouse to wake his computer. "Poor guy." He bit his lip and sighed as he waited for his accounting program to open.

Jack had started his career in fixing cars under his first boss, old Joe.

Joe was a friendly guy and great to work under. Jack could take time off whenever he needed. Customers were loyal because Joe gave them magnificent discounts. He even accepted IOUs when someone couldn't pay. They loved him and so did Jack. But the man never made much money. He was barely able to pay his only employee.

It's a mercy the man never had a family to take care of, Jack always thought to himself.

The business went under nearly two years after Jack had started working there.

It was a mess. Debts, late payments, and a host of customers' IOUs Joe didn't have the heart to collect.

Shaking the dust off his feet, Jack headed to college. When the time came for him to start his own business, he would do it right. He would be successful, profitable, and helpful—not only to his customers, but his employees as well. Beginning with no IOUs.

Getting a mechanic shop up and profitable wasn't easy, but without good cash flow he would have nothing—no growth, no money to properly pay employees, certainly no generosity or charity. Money was everything.

Jack knew making a profit required hard work, diligence, financial dexterity, and lots of grit.

Without a profit in the end you have nothing was the hard truth Jack lived by and built his business on.

And build his business he did, with three employees, a well-equipped garage, and a decent pay check not only coming to himself but to each of his employees—and all this in under four years. The business was getting by.

Yet, something gnawed at Jack. The business was getting by, but it wasn't successful. It wasn't growing as he wanted it to.

Some nights, he had trouble falling asleep. His debts haunted him. What if his business failed and he couldn't support his family? He tossed and turned, reliving the crippling poverty he and his mother had faced after his dad left them.

"There's no such thing as a plateau" he had learned in college. "If your business isn't going up, it's going down. If you're not winning, you're losing. If you're not growing, you're shrinking."

No matter how hard he worked, Jack's auto repair shop wasn't growing.

THE CLOCK read a quarter past eleven. Turning away from his computer, Jack stretched, stood, and carried the trash out to the dumpster. He noticed Wilson's Corolla sitting by the garage.

Grabbing the keys, he hopped inside the well-kept classic and pulled it into the open space.

"Needed a break," Jack replied to Pete's questioning look.

With an oil carton in one hand and a pan in the other, he got to work.

If you're not winning, you're losing, Jack. The thought nagged him every day. *Success equals profit and profit is hard work. You gotta work harder, Jack, or you'll end up like Old Joe.*

He shook his head, but the thoughts remained, hounding his mind and emotions. Jack pursed his lips again, frustration rising.

"I'll keep working harder," he mumbled to himself. "I'll make money. I'll make money and make Riley and the kids happy. Pete and Nate and Gabriel will be happy, too. I may be tough, but they'll love me in the end."

JACK STARED at his Keurig coffee sludge, swirling it slowly. His stomach twisted into knots. His heart pounded as he spoke.

"I want to help people, I think." He raised his head to look at the old man sitting across his office desk from him. He wasn't used to sharing his feelings with others, but neither did he like feeling confused. He needed to talk to someone.

"I don't think that was my motive when I first started. Then all I wanted was not to be a failure like Joe; to run a successful business, raise a happy family, and make some money. Okay, a lot of money but..." He paused and looked down at his coffee again.

His eyebrows furrowed as he pursed his lips and continued, "I think, now, I want a legacy that lasts longer than the date on my tombstone."

"Mmm." Cal nodded. "Harder than you thought, huh?" he asked in his growling bass voice.

"Don't get me wrong, the business isn't hurting—though it's certainly not growing nor is my paycheck," he explained. "My family has nothing to complain about; we have a nice house and car, even a swimming pool in the back. My wife doesn't have to work if she doesn't want to. She hangs out with her girlfriends all she wants and pursues whatever she feels like pursuing..."

He trailed off.

"But something's bothering ya deeper," the old man said. "What is it, Jack?"

"Well, it's... I think..." Jack hesitated, his cheeks glowing red with embarrassment. "It seems as though nothing is enough. I slave away at work day and night. I give my family the basic things they want. I make a decent amount of money—but it's still not enough!" He sat straighter, clenching his jaw. "And..."

"And what?"

"You wouldn't understand, Cal. I'm not sure *I* even understand. Nobody understands."

"C'mon, Jack. I know what it's like. You gotta let it out."

"How could you know? You've never run a business."

"But I have been a leader," the old man replied softly, his bass voice still growling. "And I've known businessmen all my life. I understand more than you think. And I know you will only be torn apart until you let out what's all stuck up in here." He leaned over the desk and poked the younger man in the chest.

Jack rubbed his sternum as if the poke hurt.

He looked at the old man who was waving for more coffee. Jack saw in his face—tan from years of hard work in the sun—that same old fiery passion that originally drew Jack to the man.

Jack didn't really do mentors, his ego never let him. But this old man had been there for him when no one else had been. This was the man Jack always came to with questions and the old guy always showed up, usually just to listen, sometimes to give answers. Jack could not have gotten off first base in manhood without the old man's support—let alone wooed a woman, raised a family, or ran a business.

Maybe Jack did do mentors.

"What are you feeling? Can you describe it?" the mentor asked.

"Yeah, I suppose I could, but I don't know why it matters," Jack replied.

"It matters a great deal," the old man explained. "Do you pay attention to the dash lights on your truck?"

"Of course I do."

"Your *feelings* are the dash lights of your heart and soul. Sometimes they are simply out of whack or even wrong, but most of the time they give warning to a deeper problem. You'd do very well to pay attention to your feelings, son."

"I guess I feel... I feel like I don't know what to do. Like my engine's roaring but my wheels are spinning and flinging dirt everywhere," Jack explained.

The old man set his coffee on the desk and brought his hands together up to his face, thinking.

"You know, Jack, you nee—" he began to speak but paused abruptly. "Well, let me just show you. Meet me at the cafe on Lewis next Friday—I guess that's tomorrow morning, isn't it? Be there tomorrow morning at six."

"What will I see? Is it worth my time?"

"Just come and watch, Jack." With that, Cal took one last swig of coffee, grabbed his hat, and left.

Jack was taken aback by the sudden ending to their conversation and exhaled slowly, staring blankly at his coffee again, wondering what the old guy was planning to show him.

"I hope it helps."

Noticing the time, Jack decided to let Pete close up shop. He jumped back into his Tacoma and turned the key. Nothing happened. A light on his dash caught his attention.

It flashed, "*Check Engine.*"

TWENTY-ONE MINUTES after five, Jack finally pulled into his driveway. His kids were chasing each other, giggling and laughing, around the front lawn.

He mindlessly drove past the playing kids and into his garage. He clicked the remote to shut the garage and leaned against the seat to enjoy a moment of peace before entering the kitchen.

To Jack's surprise, the kitchen contained neither wife nor supper. He searched his memory for an explanation. He found her in the living room, sitting with her back towards him, oblivious to his entrance and clearly not cooking.

Riley Martin tapped away at her computer, earbuds in, eyes down. Jack waited, annoyed by the disconnection between his expectations and reality.

Apparently still not noticing his presence or ignoring it-Jack couldn't tell-she continued working. So he did as well, resuming his routine as normal: perhaps an explanation would come to him.

When he walked out of the shower, thirty minutes later, Riley stood primping herself in front of the mirror.

"We commemorating the hungry tonight?" Jack asked sarcastically, looking at her through the mirror.

Riley furrowed her brow back at him, anger flickering in her eyes.

"Don't you remember?" she asked.

"Was I supposed to remember something?"

"Several things."

Jack pursed his lips. Work was frustrating enough. Why did he have to deal with this at home?

"The banquet tonight?" she reminded him.

Jack, groaned inwardly at himself. He bit his tongue, hard. Everything within him wanted to defend himself, but he was caught and he knew it.

He sincerely attempted to right his wrong, "I'm sorry. I forgot all about it. What time does it start?"

"Six thirty."

"Okay, we've still got time. We'll be late, but we can be ready in thirty minutes, can't we?"

"I can."

Riley's face remained unchanged in the mirror as she worked away at her hair.

"Perhaps you should apologize to your son, too," she mumbled.

Jack glared at her, more than annoyed now at her lack of response to his apology. She was referring to Jimmy's tee-ball game—the first tee-ball game of his son's life, which he had also forgotten.

The thoughts pounced immediately.

You failure! You're no better than your deadbeat dad. They're unhappy. She's unhappy. What can you do now? Nothing.

But other thoughts poured in as well: justification, anger, resentment, defense. *"She doesn't understand. Work is busy. I'm a good husband and father. She is simply ungrateful."*

"Look, I'm sorry I forgot. Let's just go to the banquet and talk about this later."

"That's okay. You're busy, I know. You don't have to come to the banquet."

Jack tried hard to restrain himself. It was bad enough to have failed twice in one day, now she was making it sound as though he didn't care about what she cared about.

"No!" he said, raising his voice. "I *want* to go to the banquet. We'll leave as soon as I'm ready."

With those words, he walked away, desperately trying to shove the anger deeper. But the despair only rose higher and consumed his thoughts.

So much for working harder, Jack Martin. You can't keep up. You're certainly not helping.

Chapter 2: Welcome to Camaraderie

JACK MADE it to the church banquet. He escorted his beautiful wife to their seats. He smiled and chatted as though everything was alright with Mr. Martin.

But inside he ran.

Despite all his big dreams and determination, his business was mediocre, his marriage dissolving into frustrations, his children (so he thought) disappointed in him, and his social life a complete facade.

He nodded and smiled as Mr. Robertson, the roofer, droned on and on about some business accountability group he had started attending.

"It's a little pricey," Mr. Robertson said, "but totally worth it. I've received really good input and support from the other business people attending."

"Oh yeah?" Jack replied placidly.

"Yeah, they helped me find solutions to some employee-related obstacles I was facing. Hey"—he seemed to have a sudden inspiration—"why don't you join us next week?" Robertson suggested.

"Oh, there's no way I'd have time." Jack surprised even himself with the indifference in his own voice.

"Well, if you ever find the time, let me know. It's worth it, man."

"Sure," was all Jack said.

THE MARTINS drove home in silence.

It was all Jack could do to hold his tongue. It was all Jack could do not to give in to the thoughts screaming in his head.

He wanted to prove himself, to compile all his arguments and level the prosecution. But Jack knew good husbands don't "level" their wives. The last thing he needed was a third strike in the good-husbandry game.

So he banished his despair to the darkest alleys of his soul.

"I'm ... I'm sorry." The words tumbled out of his mouth. He didn't look at Riley because he didn't want to see her not looking at him. "I'm sorry for forgetting..." He trailed off, waiting for some sort of acknowledgement.

It never came.

Jack clenched his teeth.

They arrived home, went to bed, and fell asleep.

"I'LL BE gone until nine tomorrow morning, Jack. Do you think you can handle the shop on your own?"

"Yes sir. Don't worry about me, Mr. Joe. I'm your man!"

Joe smiled, "Yes, you are, son. My only man."

The next morning, young Jack opened the shop on his own for the first time. It felt good, even exhilarating. For the first time, it felt like this was his shop, too, not just Joe's.

The phone rang.

"You've reached Joe's Auto Repair. This is Jack speaking. How may I help you?" he said into the telephone.

"Hi Jack!" said a sweet voice on the other side. "Is Mr. Joe there?"

"Oh, I'm sorry; he won't be in until nine o'clock. Would you like to leave a message for him?"

"Oh, well, I just needed to ask if he could spare me a little more time to make my payment. You see, it's my grandson… He needed some extra cash for college and, well…" The old lady trailed off.

"Okay, ma'am, I can leave him a message. What is your name?"

"Mrs. Jensen. Joe will know me."

Jack knew Joe couldn't afford another late payment from a customer. He wished Mrs. Jensen realized that, but it wasn't his decision.

Gulping back his frustration, he said what he knew Joe would want him to say, "I'll let him know you called, Mrs. Jensen. Can I do anything more for you?"

"No, that's all I needed. Thank you! It was nice talking to you! Ba-bye now!"

Jack squinted down at his note.

Another IOU. Another late payment. Another stunted pay check for Jack.

Jack stirred and realized he was dreaming. These days even his dreams took it upon themselves to relive the frustrations piled up within him long before college. They reminded him of why he thought the way he did. Why he believed a business was nothing without profit and, more significantly, why he was nothing without a profitable business.

He drifted back to sleep, dreaming again. But the dream changed from past memories to present torment.

"I'm disappointed in you, Jack."

Riley's face floated before him, vivid yet vague, as only dreams can do.

"Why can't you do better?"

"I'm trying!" Jack shouted in his dream. *"You just don't understand what it takes to run a business. It takes hard work, lots of hard work—and patience, Ri! But I'm trying! Just give me a break."*

"Give me a break!"

Jack jolted out of sleep. He looked around, rubbing the sleep from his eyes. The room seemed unfamiliar, as the world often seems after abruptly waking from a deep sleep.

He looked at the clock and sighed. It read *4:34 AM*, too soon to wake up, too late to get any more decent rest.

He turned to his wife, as was his habit.

She really was beautiful. And he loved her; he knew it in his head. But inwardly he still felt the confused, nondescript frustration that lingers after dreaming negatively of someone you know. He felt angry at her. And he felt angry at his anger.

Her sullenness had hurt last night. It was immature and it frustrated him. But he still loved her and he'd do anything to make her happy, even if it meant working long, hard hours.

But did she want that?

Of course she wanted the business to be successful. She certainly put a lot of work into it. But what she really wanted was him, wasn't it? She wanted him to care about her and their children. To remember them—and the things they cared about.

She wanted him to remember first tee-ball games and romantic events. Instead, he was consumed with growing his business. But what kind of husband would he be if he failed as a provider?

His employees wanted a stable paycheck, a positive future, and a boss who could afford to let them take meaningful times off for weddings. But the business Jack ran straddled such a fine financial line he could never afford to let them off or give generous bonuses.

Whatever he was doing wasn't working. One tear slid from Jack's eye as he wrestled with the clash of strangling frustration and overwhelming love.

He remembered the invitation he had to breakfast that morning. Perhaps his old friend could help him find the answers. He sure hoped so.

"JACK!" CAL called from his table, motioning him over. "Have a seat."

The young entrepreneur surveyed the scene as he made his way over to where his old friend sat.

Four others surrounded the table with the old man. One man, with hat, boots, and a large-buckled belt—obviously playing the part of the cowboy—was telling some grand story and gesticulating dramatically while the others around him listened and laughed and scoffed at the details. Something about the cowboy gave Jack a sense of *deja vu*, like he had met him before.

Another man sitting beside the cowboy, and of a considerably different size and style, rolled his eyes at the cowboy and offered his hand to Jack.

"My name is Trevor, but only officially. Please, call me Trev-unless you work for the government." The men all laughed and then introduced themselves.

These men were confident with a distinguished aura about them, as if they had done much and been much and knew it. Yet, they immediately put Jack at ease with their comfortable and casual, down-to-earth interaction. Something told him these were great men, yet he didn't recognize a single face in the group.

"Jack, these are some of my oldest friends," Cal explained.

"Yeah, you can tell by the gray hair," said the fattest who spoke with a slight Kiwi accent. Jack tried to remember his name.

"Longest lasting I mean!" Jack's old friend clarified, rolling his eyes. "Please, have a seat, Jack." He motioned to the one empty seat at the table.

The mechanic felt like a small child sitting with adults, but the men welcomed him with no hesitation, as if he were one of them.

Jack observed more than he participated in the conversation that followed. He had never seen such a group interact before. These distinguished men laughed until they cried. They told stories and reminisced together. They joked and poked fun at each other, yet affirmed each other through the twinkle in their eyes.

Soon, after the food arrived, the joking ended and the atmosphere stilled as Jack's old friend spoke up.

"Carl, how goes the project?"

"Oh, it's going fine. Just put the finishing touches on the frame this week. Now I just have to finish off the inside and get to work on the important stuff."

Jack looked inquiringly at his friend, who took the hint.

"Carl here is a former career pilot. He began in Vietnam and by the time he retired, he was flying private commercial. He likes to tinker and build things, so recently, he's been working on a project to build an airplane of his own."

Jack raised his eyebrows, speechless.

"For a customer?" he finally asked.

"No, son, I'm retired." Carl laughed. All the men laughed too, though not in a condescending way. They laughed with the amusement of older siblings when a younger brother asks a silly question.

Jack couldn't believe Carl, retired and in his upper 60s, was building an airplane.

The conversation continued with each of the men pestering Carl with questions about what exactly needed to happen next, what the costs were, whether or not the project was getting along as quickly as he had expected, and other details they apparently found interesting.

Soon it was another man's turn to share.

Jack learned that Trevor was a retired educator who currently tutored a smattering of struggling students. The man with the accent had been a career restaurateur and now ran a homeless shelter in town.

And so it went, each of them in turn sharing what they were doing and taking questions from everybody about how it was going.

Jack wasn't sure whether to be astonished, amused, or intrigued. These successful leaders and businessmen who had worked hard all their lives weren't done. They hadn't quit life to play shuffleboard for the next 20 years. They were still going, still chasing their dreams, still changing the world.

AFTER EVERYONE had told their stories, given their feedback, paid their bills, and left, Jack turned to his friend and blurted out, "What on earth was that?"

"What was what?" Cal said.

"All that!" Jack exclaimed, waving his arms in circles. "Whatever it was that just happened."

The old man laughed. "Those are my friends and comrades-in-life," he replied. "This is what I wanted to show you, Jack. I believe this is part of the answer to your questions."

"Your friends are the answer?"

"Sort of."

"I'm sorry, I don't get it." Jack wrinkled his brow.

"This group of ours has been meeting in some shape or form on and off for nearly forty years."

Jack's mouth dropped open.

"Forty years?"

"Yes sir. Apart from a couple coming and going and adding a few, this has been, for the most part, the group."

"What for? Why did you do it?" Jack questioned.

"Because we needed it. Each of us was a businessman or leader in some way. We knew we needed support, advice, and outside perspective. So we've gotten together nearly every week to eat breakfast, share a joke or two, and help each other in our endeavors. It started out as a business strategy. Now we're fast friends."

He leaned close and lowered his voice to a whisper. "Truth is we keep starting projects and building stuff just to have a reason to get together." He let out a deep chuckle.

Jack shook his head slowly.

Looking him in the eye, the old man said, "If you want your business to grow, you have to find men like this. Men who are doing stuff. Men who are learning and growing and have connections."

"That sounds ideal, but I would never have time—"

The old man stopped Jack mid-sentence. "Wait! Before you start going on about how time-consuming this is, let me explain my plan."

"Your plan?"

"Jack, yesterday you vented to me about how frustrated you were with the business. What you thought you wanted from the business was not happening. You were tired, frustrated, and angry."

"Angry? I don't recall saying—"

"I've been in your shoes, son." He interrupted Jack again. "I know that frustration. You're up against a wall you can't identify, let alone get around. It's creating a lot of friction inside of you. I saw the look in your eye. I felt it in your mood. I heard it in your voice. I know it from experience. And I know if you don't do something about it, you're going to burn-up and burn-out. But you don't know what to do."

"I certainly can't just blow a few hours every week chewing the cud with my buddies!" Jack said. "Maybe once I'm retired. But right now I have a wife and family at home. I have employees needing a consistent paycheck, suppliers needing their money. Not to mention increasing loans to pay interest on!" The words tumbled out with more heat than Jack had anticipated. He took a long breath.

"I think you're wrong. I think spending time on something like this is one of the best investments you could make," Cal said calmly. "This isn't about blowing time with your friends. These fellows are high-value men who have been places and seen things most people only dream of. Plus, we started meeting long before retirement."

"What's your plan?" Jack asked, abruptly.

"For the next five weeks, give me two hours once a week." Jack looked away as the old man explained the plan. "Just meet with me every Friday morning just like this morning. Watch the group, observe their habits, their conversations, their ideas and strategies. Once they all leave, let me tell you their stories. If after five weeks you still don't see the value in a group like this, so be it. That's fine. You can continue doing what you're doing.

"But I don't think that'll be the case. In fact, I fully expect by the end of five weeks you'll have started putting time and money into your own Winning Circle!" He grinned.

Jack looked silently at his old mentor.

"Can you do that, Jack? Is your business and your family worth it to you?"

The younger man thought for a moment.

What other choice did he have?

Chapter 3: You're Worth the Investment

"I FIRST met Carl in college. He was fresh out of 'Nam and I was a sophomore at the university. That was many years ago."

Jack listened intently as the old man gave him the rundown of how he had met Carl.

He had re-joined his mentor's group for their Friday morning routine despite his inner-resistance. Cal was right. He was desperate for a breakthrough. What other options did he have?

Now, after all the other men had left, Jack once again sat across from his old friend, listening to the first story.

"We were taking the same speech class under Professor Gorman-terribly boring," Cal said, rolling his eyes. "Neither of us learned a thing. Of course, this preceded Carl's pilot career. In fact, at the time, we were both eyeing totally different careers than we ended up pursuing.

"Anyways," he continued, "we didn't learn a thing from Gorman, but we did from each other. We sat in the back row and dreamt of all the things we would rather be doing."

The old man cleared his throat and continued with a

twinkle. "Kids these days have it easy with their iPhones. Back then we had to be very subtle when ignoring the teacher. We wrote our dreams and ideas down in our notebooks then quietly swapped replies to what the other wrote. It just looked like we were taking notes."

Cal smiled, obviously recalling fond memories. "Besides, Gorman wasn't the quickest professor on the campus," he added.

"What were you studying?" Jack asked.

"I was trying my hand at politics during those days."

Jack gaped. "You? In politics?"

"Yes!" The old man released a booming laugh. "This wasn't long after the sixties, remember. We hadn't yet discovered that not everyone is born a politician. I vainly tried to organize a team and a movement. I fantasized about starting a new party that would rise above the divisiveness of petty party politics. See my delusion already? I thought I could bring America into the new age of freedom and liberty. I figured I'd be about ready for the presidency by the turn of the century."

He laughed again.

"Carl, on the other hand, was pursuing a degree in communication." The the leftover plates shook as the old man laughed. "Imagine! Carl, a speaker? We were so young."

Jack chuckled too, more at his friend's amusement than at the thought of Carl being a speaker.

"So what happened?" he asked the old man.

"With Carl?"

"No, with your political career."

"Well, my political career would eventually fizzle out. But the party was still a work in progress"— the man settled in for the story—"which is actually where we should begin." He said with a twinkle in his eye, "Jack, you know a lot already. You understand the basics of business?"

"I've spent four years building my business, so, yeah, I would say so."

"Means less groundwork for us to cover. If you really want to excel in business-or as a leader, period-one of the first thing you need to learn is the importance of contribution. So I'm going to tell you today what I learned from Carl about contribution."

"Contribution?" Jack repeated, glancing down at his smartphone.

"Yes, contribution. But I don't mean contribution like paying into a financial kitty. I'm talking about contributing something much more valuable than money. I'm talking about the contribution of ... well..." The old man looked at Jack's phone. "I guess you probably don't have time for this story," he said with mock self-pity.

Dropping his phone, Jack pulled his arms together and leaned in.

"Sorry." He smiled sheepishly. "I am interested. I want to hear."

Cal straightened. "Good," he said, eyeing Jack with a mischievous grin. He lifted his mug as the waitress poured him more coffee.

"As I said, my political career wouldn't last long. However, the team—the party some of us were building—had struck a chord with other students. People wanted in on it. They wanted to hear our ideas and discuss them. It was great, but the structure was fragile. We were beginning to fracture.

"My bull-headed opinions and fist-pounding sermons certainly didn't help anything. People liked being a part of the discussions. They liked the setting, but I think they found it hard to follow me as a leader. I enjoyed hearing my own opinions and hated being challenged or put in my place. I was a one man show.

"People started grumbling—you know how that happens. One off-hand comment about bad leadership and next thing you know everybody's talking about all the problems. Of course, no one talks to the people who actually need to hear the feedback so they can change."

"Gossip," Jack mumbled.

"You know what I'm talking about?"

"Yes, I do."

"It's an awful thing, but that's a whole other story." The old man waved the topic aside. "Once I got wind of the grumblings, I immediately started taking steps to solve the problem. But instead of going to trusted friends and advisors as I should have done—you know, people like Carl or even the actual people doing the grumbling—I went to this 'great', 'ground-breaking' seminar on leadership and teamwork."

"You had those back then?" Jack asked.

"Son, this was the '70s, the days of enlightenment and the dawn of the new age. We invented self-help seminars! At first I loved it. They gave me all kinds of resources—workbooks, motivational tapes, and the like. It all made me feel good for a while, but never made a long-lasting impact.

"I would get so frustrated. Sometimes I was frustrated with myself for investing so much money and time into those crazy seminars. Then I'd get frustrated at the guys selling the seminars and writing the books. What rip-offs! Some days, I was angry and frustrated for no particular reason. I felt stuck with the whole political party and leadership thing. I felt like all the energy I put into making myself better was going to waste.

"Looking back now, I realize that their material was ineffective because it was incomplete. You always needed to join one more program or buy another book or something even more expensive."

"Hasn't changed a bit," Jack interjected.

The old man shook his head. "Yeah, I found out real quick that most 'business' or 'leadership' seminars promising success were overpriced and ultimately unhelpful. Most of the time they just didn't align with my values."

Jack nodded in agreement.

"You know what I mean, huh?" Cal chuckled. "Although I realized they weren't always worth their price, I did learn some things during that time. One thing I learned was that you don't have to apply every single thing from every single seminar or book. All you need to do is learn one or two things you can apply really well.

"At the end of the day, though," he continued, "what I really found helpful were those conversations with Carl. The back row note-swapping sessions were much more effective than any of those expensive seminars.

"You know," he said, suddenly reminiscent, "Carl had this way of putting people at ease by asking questions. This always got them to talk. My political buddies and I just argued and defended ourselves, but Carl gently pulled ideas from people and allowed them a place at the table, so to speak."

He paused, setting his mug down and looking up at the vine-entangled lattice, which shaded the cafe courtyard.

"The real breakthrough for me came one time when Carl was especially blunt with me. We were trading notes again in Professor Gorman's class. I had written a long soliloquy about some idea a fellow student had shared in our party meeting and how stupid I thought it was."

Jack's mentor reached into his pocket and pulled out what

looked like a folded photocopy of an old notebook leaf. He unfolded it and began to read.

"'Do you think he's really the stupid one?' Carl wrote back. 'Sure, his ideology may be naive, but don't you think, if you look closely, there's gold under the naivety? There always is. You just have to mine it out. If you immediately reject the ideas people offer you, you'll never produce a refined idea. You'll have no revelations, no light bulb moments, no innovation, just the ideas in your own head because you don't think anyone else has anything to offer. Truth be told, bud, the ideas in your head won't change the world. It takes a team.'"

"Ouch!" Jack empathized. "That must've hurt."

"Well, I got over it," the old man said dismissively. "What Carl was talking about was *contribution*, the contribution of ideas and criticism. You can't light a fire with one stick or a single match. You need *two* sticks or *two* flints, a match *and* a striker. The same is true for any type of venture, whether a political party, a non-profit, a church, a family, or-most certainly-a business like yours. You can't do this alone. You need contribution. You need people to push back against your ideas against in order to make a spark. You need to do business within a strong community."

He paused to let Jack think about it.

After a moment, Jack straightened. "This all sounds ideal," he said, "but I just don't have time for it. I have so much to do: paperwork, follow-up calls, let alone the actual mechanic work. I can't do it."

"There you go again." The old man sighed. "That's what I said at first too. But, as Carl told me, 'If you want to facilitate a successful movement you gotta strategize—together, with other people. Get the ones most committed and creative to start having meetings with you.'

"I resisted at first. I could barely split my time between politics and homework and all the other activities I was already involved with. Strategy meetings sounded like just one more thing to add to my busy schedule.

"Nevertheless, I was passionate about this movement. I wanted to make it a success and I knew Carl was right. I knew if we were going to make a difference in our political sphere, I had to start allowing everyone's voice to be heard—even the ones I most disagreed with.

"I knew it would take time. But I also knew if I didn't take it seriously, I would be waving our beloved party—and any hope of change—goodbye. So I did it. I plunged in."

"How did you do it?" Jack asked.

"I started by taking a hard look at every activity I participated in—the things eating up my time. I eliminated anything I was not passionately committed to. I saw change needed to happen and I chased after it. I only kept my studies, the party, and the activities that actually re-energized me.

"I organized strategy meetings. I included more people in our discussion times. I argued less and listened more. I surveyed the student body as a whole and our political party specifically. I got feedback.

"Soon, it stopped being all *'I'* and *'my'* and became *'us'* and *'ours'*. It grew into a true movement and people loved it. Even after I realized politics wasn't my calling and left, 'The Party'—as we called it—was alive and well and making a meaningful difference too."

"And you think this happened because you started meeting with other people and really listening to them?" Jack asked.

"It certainly facilitated the change."

"Well, I'm glad it all worked out for your party," Jack said. "But I'm just a mechanic. I'm not a politician. I'm not working with ideas or people. I'm working with cars and tools. They don't give much feedback."

"Oh, but you do work with people, Jack. You have employees, don't you? You have customers. You have a family and neighbors, friends, a church. You do work with people and ideas. If you want your business to grow, you have to start valuing contribution. When you're stuck in quicksand, struggling on your own only pushes you in deeper. You need friends to help you out of quicksand."

"So you think if I just get together with some friend to talk about my business it could grow?"

"Not exactly. I'm saying being involved in a community of mutual giving—contribution—is where successful leaders spring from. It doesn't just involve talking about *your* business. It involves contributing your ideas to *theirs* as well. You grow by contributing to other people and them to you. Plus, it involves growing *personally*."

"Personally? You mean like some sort of life coaching program?" Jack scoffed.

Cal nodded without batting an eye. "If you don't grow yourself, Jack, how in the world do you expect to grow your business?" The old mentor continued, "Things go on beneath the surface that keep you from generating your best work. You know that deep down. You just won't admit it yet."

Jack squirmed in his seat.

"Did this Friday-morning-group-accountability-thing that you're still doing come out of your political party?" he asked, changing the subject.

He was beginning to feel uncomfortable. Cal was digging too deep. They both knew it. Jack's thick veneer hid a frightened little boy. Alone and afraid, his soul shuddered at the idea of being found out. So he skirted around the real issues to distract the old man from what was really going on inside.

The mentor eyed Jack tenderly. He saw a new fire blazing in the younger man's eyes, whether good or bad, he couldn't tell yet. He felt compassion for the mechanic because he had been there, too, many years ago. He would let Jack play his little games for now, but eventually Jack would need to tear away the veneer or he would suffocate.

"Oh, no!" the old man said. "No, Carl wasn't much interested in politics. Neither was I, to be honest, it just took me some time to figure that out. No, this group came out of those note-trading sessions in the back of Professor Gorman's class. Little did we know what started out as just a couple of bored students was only the beginning."

"The beginning of what?" Jack asked.

The old man spread out his arms as if to include the whole table.

"The beginning of an invaluable relationship between the two of us lasting over forty years, eventually including all of these fine gentlemen you've been getting to know."

"I see," Jack said.

"Everything I know about contribution and collaboration came from Carl. Don't know where he learned it, but he did. Somewhere, somehow." Cal shrugged. "If I hadn't listened to him and asked him questions and if he hadn't been bold enough to offer his advice, all of his wisdom and experience would have gone untapped—at least by me."

Jack began to respond, but his old mentor continued.

"I learned many things about leadership and business through starting a political movement," he said. "But two things in particular stand out to me. First"—he held up his finger—"you must learn from your peers and comrades, like we've been talking about. Second, there is no greater teacher than experience, both your own and that of others. Almost all of this learning happens in the context of strong community."

Jack watched as the waitress started clearing their breakfast dishes.

Looking at his mentor, he said, "I've known you all these years and yet have never heard this. I didn't even know about this group of friends. Why didn't you tell me?"

"You never asked."

Jack tilted his head to the side. It was true, he hadn't asked. He had just plunged into business and never once thought to ask his old friend.

"Why didn't you ever go into business if you knew so much about it?" he asked Cal.

"Well..." He gazed off, past the cafe and morning traffic jamming Lewis Street. He seemed to be looking at something a long way off. But Jack could see nothing beyond the opposing shops. "I was meant to do something else, I guess." He grinned mildly.

Jack opened his mouth to ask another question, but the old man stopped him.

"Oh, that's enough for today," he said, stretching and yawning again. "Keep your eyes open this week. All around you there is plenty of untapped potential and untapped wisdom and experience. Look for it. Seek it out. Learn from it. Next week, perhaps we'll talk about Kip."

"Kip? The restaurateur?"

"That's the one. By the end of his career, he was only working three days a week."

Incredulous, Jack began to mock the idea, but Cal held up his hands.

"Next week, Jack. I'll tell it all."

Chapter 4: Win With Fewer Hours

"JACK, YOU have to start working fewer hours."

Jack's friend started their second week with a bombshell.

"Work fewer hours?" Jack retorted. "I think all this analytical mumbo-jumbo has gone to your head, Cal."

They both chuckled.

"Naw, I'm serious, Jack! You need to shed this mindset of 'Work hard, work long; take no time off'."

"But that's business! It's hard work. It takes long hours," the younger man rejoined, sounding more confident than he really was.

The old man looked him square in the eye for a moment before asking, "How's that workin' for ya?"

Jack fidgeted with his napkin. Truth was, it wasn't working out for him—not in the way he had hoped.

"But..." he stammered, "but ... there's more than that to my problems. That's not what's holding me back." He paused before adding, "Is it?"

"Being addicted to work is a real problem. It's not the cause of everything. But it is definitely a big part of it," he repeated.

Jack gazed out the window and across the street where the proprietor of a flower shop was just opening his doors.

Although he felt more and more comfortable sharing his struggles with his mentor, it still made him nervous. Exposing embarrassing weaknesses and frustrations wasn't exactly his favorite pastime. He didn't like admitting ignorance of anything, let alone business.

"How could hard work and long hours be bad for my business? That doesn't make any sense."

"Oh, hard work isn't bad. The issue at hand is using your time efficiently. Let me ask you this-who processes the bills at your shop?"

"I do," Jack replied.

"Is that what you envisioned doing when you opened a mechanic shop, processing bills?"

"No, of course—"

"Why did you open your mechanic shop, Jack?"

"To work on cars, to do what I love, what I'm good at, and to provide some security for me and my family," Jack answered. These felt like simpleton questions, which annoyed him.

"Do you love processing your bills? Do you love running payroll? Do you love running to AutoZone for small, forgotten parts?"

"Of course not, but it's a necess—"

"Then why are you still spending long hours processing all that paperwork, Jack?"

Jack furrowed his brow and pursed his lips, silent but pondering, trying to figure the old man out.

Folding his weathered hands and resting them on his stomach, Cal nestled back into his chair. It was story time.

"Kip struggled with this exact same problem," the mentor explained. "As a kid, he'd spend hours pretending to serve customers while waiting for his dad to come home. That's where he got his passion to run a restaurant himself. He got his energy and grit from his dad."

"Where'd he get his raw approach to relationships?" Jack asked.

The older man narrowed his eyes. "You've observed him well. His parents divorced when he was five. I know few men who have worked harder than Kip during their careers. Unfortunately, that drive and raw way of relating-as you say-is what tore his own family apart."

"Oh?" Jack raised his brow. "I didn't realize he had family."

"Not many do. His work ethic destroyed it."

Jack straightened, now actually interested.

"By nature, the man doesn't know how to stop. He's a workaholic—or rather he used to be. He learned the hard way that success isn't all about money.

"Kip came to Colorado during the '60s, trying to get away from the pill-popping, surf-riding hippie crowd his brother and sister had fallen in with. They sought meaning through drugs and pleasure. Kip looked for it through money and success.

"He determined to make something of himself and follow his dreams. That was his life. That's what defined him.

"I met him in '74, in one of his restaurants. At the time it was his only establishment. I was barely out of college and ready to take on the world. There I was, eating a delicious steak at this new place in the river city. Suddenly, through the kitchen doors bounded this young, well-built, fireball of a man.

"The guy shot like lightning through the room and never stopped. 'Hey, you do this,' he would tell an employee. 'Don't forget this,' he told another. 'Waitress, you'll have to cover these guests.' Go, go, go. He never stopped

"I wanted to meet this alien force of a man. So, at one point in the evening, when he landed for air, I took the chance to introduce myself.

"All I managed to get out of him was a long run-on sentence. 'Name's Kip, sir. Very nice to meet you; hope you enjoyed yourself. Come again! Sorry, can't chat; lots to do when running a new business, ya know.' Next thing I knew, he had scurried off to continue his managing. I thought right then and there, *This man will self-destruct very quickly if he doesn't stop for a breath.*

"Anyways, so every time I went through, I stopped in at Kip's for a nice, juicy steak and a chance to catch the fireball and talk with him. Kip lived by the dangerous idea that in order to make his restaurant a success, he had to work long, dreadful hours.

"I remember one night—after a few months of getting to know each other pretty well—I caught him closing up the shack all by himself.

"'What're your plans for the rest of the evening, Kip?' I asked. 'Do you enjoy bowling? I think there's an alley not too far from here.'

"'Ah, there is—up three blocks. I suppose I'd enjoy it, I just never have the time,' he responded. He barely even looked up from his paperwork—bills and such, by the look of it.

"'Gotta sweep this floor—it's a mess—after I've finished up this paperwork. Then I got some other random bitties to do yet before I go home to the miss.'

"I nearly fell over from shock right in front of him. He was going to sweep the floor himself, and he also had a wife waiting for him at home!

"'Sounds incredibly busy, man,' I told him.

"'It's all part of being an entrepreneur, man,' he replied.

"'Couldn't you get one of your employee's to sweep the floor,' I asked.

"'Why should they if I can do it?' he asked.

"Like I said, Kip was incredibly driven. He loved serving people, crafting delicious food, and making money doing it. There was no other industry for him. But just like you, he carried this dangerous 'My business won't succeed unless I work long hours' mindset."

"But isn't that just reality?" Jack inserted. "Isn't that part of the toll of being an entrepreneur?"

"You're right." The old man surprised Jack by agreeing with him. "It is part of the toll. It's hard work to get a business off the ground. It often demands long hours from you. But driving yourself—and the people around you—nutty by working crazy hours doesn't guarantee success. Like I've been saying, it's usually the quickest route to disaster."

He let Jack ponder the thought.

"Let me give you an example from Kip's life.

"The longer I got to know him the more my suspicions were confirmed. This man was drunk on work and in perilous danger of a bad crash. In fact, he told me once he didn't feel satisfied with himself unless he put in at least sixty hours a week at the restaurant. He was measuring his success by how many hours of work he put in!" The old man slapped his hands on the table in exclamation before continuing. "About two years into the venture, Kip hit a major plateau, much like where you're at today. The business was surviving, but the work was hard and he was wearing out. This took a toll on everyone around him.

"His most discouraging moment came after working eight

days in a row. Understandably, his wife was not excited about these work hours and was trying to get his attention. This particular night, despite his exhaustion, they argued long past midnight.

"I remember his call clearly:

"'She wants a divorce, Cal,' he told me. 'Says she's done with living alone. Says I can't be married to her and the restaurant. She just doesn't understand.'"

"And what did you say?" interrupted Jack.

"I didn't know what to say. At this point, I had known him for less than a year. I knew he was running a destructive lifestyle, but didn't know it had come to this.

"'Kip,' I said, 'Take a few days off, the restaurant will be fine. Give her some space, but take time to talk with her, hear her out. Try to listen, Kip. I'll be up the day after tomorrow and I'm bringing Carl with me, okay? We're here for you, man.'

"So we came. We had no clue what to tell him, but we knew he had to change his lifestyle, especially if he wanted to save his marriage, but even to save his business.

"He kept on telling us it was so hard and grueling but that he loved it. It was what kept him going. He told us the hardest part was his personal life. He claimed he and his wife had been fighting every day."

The old man's eyes began to fill with tears as he told his friend's story.

"Then he asked me how he could survive without his work?"

The old man paused and shook his head.

"'How can I survive without my work?' That's what he said, Jack. He wasn't asking, 'How can I survive without my wife? How can I survive without sleep? He needed his work more than his wife—the woman he once loved more than anything else, the person who was supposed to be his *partner* in life!"

"We listened; we questioned; we tried to understand his situation. This struggle was obviously tearing him apart. He lacked the support only those closest to him could give, and was even experiencing rejection in place of it. And all of it was only driving him to work *harder*.

"Carl was the one who finally confronted the real issue head on. I was too worried about hurting Kip's feelings.

"'Kip, you've got to slow down,' Carl insisted. 'You're destroying yourself.'

"I still remember Kip's confused look.

"'But my business needs me. I can't afford to slow down!' he said.

"'You can't afford this plateau you're on, either. You can't afford to micromanage your employees. You can't afford to lose your soul mate.

"'The real problem is that you can't afford *not* to slow down. Most of this stuff you're doing isn't worth your time.'

"'Well, someone has to do it!' he threw back."

Cal paused, before saying with a wink, "Sounds familiar, now that I think about it."

Jack rolled his eyes.

"We agreed with Kip that someone had to do it. 'But it shouldn't be you,' Carl told him. 'You're the leader. You are the vision and soul of the restaurant. You spearhead the way; you set the course; you call the shots.' Then we asked him what we ask every business owner: Why he started the restaurant to begin with.

"'Because I love making delicious food and seeing people happy,' he replied.

"Carl told him he should be spending most of his time on just that-creating delicious meals, delighting customers with a quality experience, and finding new and better ways to do it.

"That's when I piped in. I told Kip, 'Your job is to move the business forward and upward. That's where your time is most profitable. Don't throw it away on minimum wage chores.'

"I could see the light bulb beginning to flicker."

"'And you must take care of your allies: your wife and those closest to you. They're your lifesavers. If you create an incredible business but destroy your family by your crazy hours and lifestyle, you haven't succeeded at anything.'"

"Kip pondered it all for a long moment. I could sense the internal battle raging within him. Everything he lived for, everything that gave him a will and drive to live was wrapped up in his business."

Cal looked at Jack.

Silence enveloped the cafe and they sat quietly for a moment. Jack tried to process everything the old man had just told him.

"It just doesn't sound right," he finally said. "'Work fewer hours, get more done.'"

"Goes against everything you thought you knew, doesn't it?" the old man agreed.

"There's a rule, for this," he continued, "I think they call it the eighty-twenty rule or something like that these days. Perhaps you've heard of it? It's supposed to help us understand a bunch of stuff we need to know about life and business. But for us right now the issue at hand is *time*. What do you spend your time doing?" he asked.

"What do you mean?" Jack asked.

"All day, every day, what do you do?"

"I mean ... I try to be at work at least by six o'clock every morning, if not sooner. I usually eat breakfast before I go or I pick something up on my way. We open the garage at eight, so I have plenty of time to work on paperwork or any vehicles before customers start arriving."

"How much time do you spend on paperwork?"

"Couple hours a day total maybe."

"And is that why you opened a mechanic shop?"

"No, of course it's not."

"Is it important for *you* to do all the paperwork or can anybody do paperwork?"

"I suppose anyone could," Jack consented.

"Good. Anyways, continue explaining your routine. Do you ever do errands, run for tools or parts—that kind of thing?"

"Sometimes throughout the day or on my way home from work, yeah, I'll pick something up."

"When customers drive into *'Jack's Auto Repair'*, who do you think they expect to meet?" the old man questioned.

"Well, me—"

"JACK!" his mentor interrupted. "They expect to meet *Jack*. But are they going to meet Jack if he's off running to AutoZone for another carton of oil?"

"We ... we buy it in bulk," Jack corrected.

Cal waved it off with a chuckle. "Whatever you get at AutoZone then. Doesn't matter. What does matter is that your customers meet the guy whose name is on the sign. It's important they find the trustworthy guy running the place and have confidence he's the one working on or at least overseeing those working on their car. It doesn't matter who runs the errands, does it?"

"Well, sometimes we have to find particularly unique parts."

"But that's not hard. You can train the other guys to do that pretty well, can't you?"

He didn't wait for an answer, but continued on. "Here's the thing, Jack. Spend your precious time working on stuff that drives your business forward. Interact with the customers to build trust. Work on their cars and do a good job so they keep coming back. Find ways to get them talking about your shop in a better light than the next guy's shop. Train the other employees to be five-star mechanics. And stop messing around doing odd jobs any of your men could do. Hire a secretary, assign one of the guys to be an errand-boy—do stuff to lighten your load.

"Is this making sense, son? The idea is to make a lifelong habit of letting go of the 'low value' things. Focus on doing things only you can do to drive the business forward. Leave the rest for your employees. That's why you hired them. Kip realized most of the stuff he was working long hours to get done could have been done by someone else. So why put in ridiculous hours when you could be spending more time doing stuff that actually grows your business and with your wife and kids?"

The old man leaned in as he finished up his little speech.

Jack fiddled with a leftover piece of toast from breakfast and sat in silence. The old man waited patiently for him to process everything.

"So that's how Kip learned to work only three days a week?" he asked Cal.

"Yup, by doing the stuff only he could do and having others do the rest."

Jack watched a couple of sparrows swoop in to pick up the crumbs scattered by the men that morning. The eight o'clock sun penetrated the previously shadowy atmosphere and began to warm them as they sat silently.

"Slow down, work fewer hours, maximize whatever makes you most productive..."

This was a hard turn for Jack to make. Everything he thought he had learned from years of running his own business—let alone the training he had gotten in college— turned out to be wrong.

He looked up at his old mentor. Did this man really know what he was talking about or were these just mere opinions he was reading into his experience?

"What happened then?" he asked the old man.

"To what?" Cal grunted in reply.

"To Kip. Did he change?"

"Kip?" he said, perking up. "He didn't change overnight. He was addicted to his work, you know. Most people can't kick their addictions overnight. But he did change eventually. And it probably saved his life and his business. Unfortunately, it was too late to save his marriage. She was hurt, angry, and fed up, so she packed her bags and left."

"Is she still around?"

"They maintained a civil relationship—for the sake of the kids, mostly. But she remarried and seemed to have a happy life until she passed away about seven years ago."

"Did Kip ever remarry?"

"Nope. No, he loved only Olivia, deep in his heart. He just didn't realize it until it was too late. He had been too busy to see she no longer loved him."

JACK THOUGHT of Kip and Olivia the entire ride home.

Kip's words haunted him, *'How can I survive without my work?'*

How do I survive? Jack wondered.

He had spent so many years believing he would be a failure if he didn't make his business profitable; he couldn't imagine thinking any other way. As small as it was, mechanics was his life. The thought of giving some of his work to another person terrified him.

But what did Cal know? He wasn't a businessman. What gave him the right to make such strong assertions about how Jack should run his business?

It was late in the afternoon now. Jack began his evening jog by walking vigorously down the driveway from his house. Getting outside and exercising always cleared his mind.

He picked up his pace and broke into a jog. His heart fluttered a little as he caught sight of Riley walking up to the house from working in the garden. He always thought she was especially cute in work clothes.

Saving his family was a no-brainer. Of course he wanted that. Only an idiot would decisively choose to hurt his family.

But would working long hours to build a successful business really tear them apart?

Stop running errands to AutoZone. Do the stuff only you can do to drive your business forward. Let go of doing 'low-value' activities yourself.

Jack broke into a run down the street, eyes narrowed in on the path in front of him. The breeze against his face was a familiar sensation and the mix of emotions took him right back to that terrible day so many years ago.

JACK REMEMBERED the branches scraping his cheeks as the mist rose up from the forest floor mixing with the smells and sounds of lilies and moss and little Muffin barking after him. Suddenly, his foot had slipped in the mud and he had fallen face first into thick, wet earth. Searing pain shot up his arm and tears flowed hot down his cheeks.

"DADDY-Y-Y!" he cried. "MA-A-MMA!"

"HELLO! ANYBODY home?" Riley asked her husband, who now sat on the porch stairs.

"I'm sorry. What did you say?" Jack said, emerging from his thoughts.

"I've been standing here trying to get your attention. What were you thinking about?"

"Oh, just my conversation with Cal." He wiped the sweat off his brow. "What did you want?"

"I was wondering if you could help me in the garden at some point. I need that old fence stake pulled out," his wife repeated.

"Oh." Jack thought for a moment. "I mean, yeah, I guess I can do that. I don't know when, but I can help you out."

He knew it wasn't the right answer. But he didn't feel up to a cheerful, "Yes! I'd be happy to." He had plenty on his mind already. This fence stake surely wasn't more important than any of the other tasks calling his name.

"Well, if you don't have time to help me, don't worry about it." She stood for a moment, obviously hurt, then walked into the house.

The roar of a mower and the sound of his children playing with the neighbor kids wafted across the yard. It was a peaceful late summer evening outside, but he didn't notice.

Inside Jack Martin a different sound filled the air: a little boy screaming for help, lost in the woods, calling for a daddy who never came. He clenched his fist shut as if to grasp an invisible foe.

YET ANOTHER FAILURE! the thoughts yelled. *Oh, she hates you even more now.*

She doesn't understand what I'm going through, he told himself. *She doesn't understand the pressure.*

The faint gurgle of boiling water came from the otherwise silent kitchen.

"Riley!" he called out. "Something's on the stove!"

No answer.

His mentor's words rang in his ear, *"How much is your family worth to you?"*

He knew he was in the wrong. He knew Cal was right. He knew he should apologize. Again. But humble pie is especially hard to swallow twice.

In the long run, she was more important than his business and most certainly more important than his pride. In the long run.

But not at the moment.

Chapter 5: You're Not Alone

"GOODBYE kids! See you next month!" Mr. Young said to his students as they ran out the door. "Goodbye!" one shouted back. None said, "Thank you!" Most didn't even acknowledge his presence.

The first year teacher shut the door and sank down into his chair, exasperated from the long, strenuous week and month and year. He could still hear the rush of students running out the front entrance, voices cheering for the holidays, feet stomping down the hall, doors slamming shut.

Mr. Young wondered whether a career in teaching had been a mistake. So far it had been miserable. He went over the day, trying to figure out what he could have done better, how he could have calmed the unruly fourth grade men vying for leadership. Encouraging giggles from girls was clearly a much higher priority for nine and ten-year-old boys than the history lesson or its teacher.

No matter, the Christmas season had arrived, which meant a two-and-a-half week break before he would have to compete again for the attention of the little fourth grade warriors and giggling queens.

The young teacher closed his eyes as the noise from the halls quieted. He sighed with relief at the thought of two weeks home alone with his own queen. And tomorrow he would join his comrades for one last breakfast before the break. That was good. He enjoyed getting together with his new business friends. He liked the perspective they brought to his life and fledgling career, even though sharing his struggles always scared him. Perhaps they could help him solve this fourth-grade riddle.

"MORNING, JACK!" Cal exclaimed at the arrival of his friend.

Jack stopped, frowned, and stared at the empty table. Since he was usually the last one to arrive, it confused him that his old friend sat alone at their table.

"Where's everybody else?" he inquired.

"They all had other things going on, so I guess it's just you and me today."

"Okay," Jack said with an amused grin. "Fine with me. So what are we talking about this morning?"

"Your friends!" the old man said cheerfully.

"My friends? What about my friends?"

"Can you talk to them?"

"Well, I talk to you, don't I?" Jack threw back.

Cal chuckled. "Oh, mercy, what a boring life you must lead!"

Jack grinned to himself as he looked over the menu.

"No, I mean your peers—people young enough to still be doing life and business; your friends who *didn't* watch the moon landing. Are you able to talk to them about stuff?"

"Yeah, I talk to them, I guess."

"He guesses." The old man grumbled to the waitress just walking up.

"I'll have my usual, Connie," he told her. "And you're paying," he informed the younger man.

"Oh, really now?" Jack raised his eyebrows in mock surprise.

They finished ordering and continued their conversation.

"You have to understand; I don't know very many people who face the same kind of problems that I do," Jack confessed. "Nobody will understand anyway, so how could it be helpful to talk about my struggles?"

"How do you know no one will understand? Have you tried?"

Jack thought for a while.

"It's just ... a lot of the people at church don't know what it takes to run a repair shop. My neighbors don't talk to each other, so I don't really know them. And most of my business friends don't understand why I value church or family or people like you." The old man laughed heartily.

"Most people don't understand people like me," he said. "I'm used to it by now."

The waitress set their drinks in front of them.

"But have you ever actually taken them out for coffee and shared your stories and struggles and listened to theirs?" the old man asked.

Jack shrugged. "I guess not."

"You might be surprised who actually does understand you. That's what happened with Trev."

"Trev from your group? I was wondering when we'd get to him."

"Yup. When he first started coming, it scared him out of his mind to share his struggles."

Jack nodded in agreement. "No kidding."

"Trev was struggling with a problem that really had him stumped and depressed. Barely four months into his teaching career, he already felt burned out and at his wits' end. He even questioned whether he should've been teaching at all.

"He had hesitated to share his struggles all fall because it embarrassed him to be so helpless in solving a problem he should have been able to fix—as a trained teacher and all.

"But the thing that really got him down was the nagging doubt about whether he had chosen the right career. Imagine it; he questioned a choice that had affected the last four and a half years of his life. It embarrassed him.

"Finally, having tried everything for an entire semester, he determined to bring up both his problem and his restlessness at our final meeting before Christmas. He was still working up the courage to spill out his guts when Carl told us a story from the cockpit. Of all people, it connected with Trev."

"DID I ever tell you how I learned to manage my energy during long commercial flights?" the pilot asked.

The young teacher leaned in. He had determined to share everything with this group of wise men, namely, his embarrassingly small problem of keeping the attention of fourth-grade students. He also decided, at the strong encouragement of his wife, to share his regret over becoming a teacher.

But at this point, he was relieved to have a few extra moments of reprieve while the pilot, Carl, recounted one of his many stories. Sharing always terrified him. None of these guys were teachers: how could they understand his problem? Besides, they were all smart and experienced. It embarrassed him to admit to struggling over an issue for so long with so little improvement.

"So, I struggled to keep my energy levels up for many years after becoming a commercial pilot," Carl was saying. "I didn't face it as much during the war, so I didn't learn how to deal with it.

"One flight to London was especially bad. I was drinking coffee and peeing so much that the attendants started giggling every time I left the cockpit. You can imagine how my co-pilot made fun of me!

"From that point on, I began searching for a solution to my problem. Airlines didn't have a lot of protocol when it came to this kind of stuff back then, so I had to figure it out on my own.

"I started by cutting out all television in the evenings before my flights. At first, I cut it out every other flight and recorded how I slept the nights I watched television versus the nights I didn't. And I logged how I felt throughout the following flights and so on. I kept track like this for several months and began noticing a subtle difference.

"The nights I watched television, it took me longer to settle down and fall asleep. Subsequently, it took me longer to wake up the next morning as well. The days and flights following were groggier in general—not significantly, but when I noticed them week after week in my journal, there was definitely a pattern.

"After I concluded that not watching television improved my sleep, I tried two other things that especially improved my energy during long flights.

"I started avoiding newspapers the morning of my flight, and instead spent that time either exercising or reading for pleasure to relax my brain instead of working it.

"I began eating nutrient rich meals beforehand: lots of

meat, vegetables, and fruits. I also made sure to snack well during the flight; instead of drinking soda and coffee, I began drinking primarily water.

"No more dozing off during those long flights after that. I slept like a rock at night, too." Carl concluded.

Listening to Carl explain what he learned about managing his energy, Trev suddenly had an idea about how to help his kids stay engaged in his class.

Perhaps their problem wasn't that his lessons weren't engaging enough (though that certainly may have been part of it). Perhaps their problem was pent up energy mixed with tiredness which distracted them from focusing on the lesson.

He could chalk it up to being merely fourth-grade antics. But perhaps a lack of proper exercise, fresh-air, and restful sleep combined with fourth-grade restlessness rendered their minds incapable of focusing on the lesson.

He concluded their minds were tired but their bodies energetic.

"SUDDENLY, OUR young teacher felt a new energy and vigor for his class and career. He now had a theory that could possibly not only resolve his frustration, but actually *help* the children and their parents," Cal explained.

"How did he do it?" Jack asked.

"Like Carl, he started with television. He figured it was the primary problem among his kids, so so he thought getting that out of the way should be his first priority.

"Here's what he did. Each student who could verify they hadn't watched any TV or played Nintendo the previous night went home with no homework."

Jack's mouth dropped open, "No homework?" he exclaimed.

"With no homework. He believed paying attention in class was more important than whatever they'd learn through homework. Furthermore, if they could bring proof from friends or family that they spent significant time playing or working outside, they received extra credit. All he asked was parents or guardians to sign a note .

"He found this worked quite effectively with most of the kids. Of course there were the couch potatoes who liked their TV, but even they usually found it hard to turn down a chance to skip homework.

"He also petitioned the school to provide healthier but tasty meals, which proved harder than he anticipated. In the end, though, they saw the value and tried his experiment. He made nutritious snacks a routine part of the classroom. He fostered all of these new measures by giving incentives such as no homework, extra field trips, free days, and the like.

"It's amazingly simple, but releasing the pent-up energy by encouraging physical exercise helped all of them, especially the couch potatoes, to have dramatically increased attention spans. They improved even to the point that even kids who had been failing started getting C's. Along with this, the students were much more responsive to his attempts at reining them in—even when the girls were giggling at the boys.

"Wow!" Jack exclaimed. "That's quite cutting edge for—when was this, the eighties?"

"Yup. Trev's an innovator at heart," the old man agreed. "But he was only interested in helping the kids."

The breakfast arrived and the two men started eating.

"You say, Jack, people can't understand your problems. Your problems are too unique. But who's more different from each other than a teacher and an airline pilot?"

"They're certainly different," Jack agreed, taking a bite out of his toast.

"Yes, they certainly are. Yet a random story from the cockpit spawned an incredible breakthrough for a *teacher*. Never underestimate the experiences of your friends and peers, Jack. You never know who you might learn from. Who knows, you might even learn about your business from me!" The old man chuckled as he dove into his eggs and hash browns.

Cal continued speaking, despite the food in his mouth. "Trev's school became one of the most successful in developing healthy, smart students as a direct result of his initiatives. Grades went up while the amount of time spent in detention and suspensions went down. Trev was a good fifteen years ahead of himself and is now an award-winning teacher."

Wiping the corners of his mouth, the old mentor looked at Jack and grinned "It was all because he involved himself in a strong community of thinkers and doers."

"Speaking of doing," Jack said, "I need you to come help me remove a stake in our garden tonight."

"Oh?" the older man said, interested. "You want the old buffer to come throw his back out?"

"No, I need strong community to give me moral support while I sweat my brains out," Jack said with a twinkle in his eye. "Besides, it's been awhile since you were at our place for dinner. It's time you came over again."

"I'd love to."

"STRONG COMMUNITY," Jack stated through heavy breaths. "You've mentioned it several times now."

"Yup," Cal grunted as he shoveled dirt away from the stake.

"What do you mean? What is it?" Jack asked.

"It's everything," his mentor said, "everything we've been talking about the last few weeks. It's your friends, the people you go on the adventure of life with-your partners, your family, your wife."

The old man paused, noticing Jack's hesitation at the mention of his wife.

He leaned on his shovel and asked, "Somethin' wrong between you and Riley?"

"Ah, it's nothing," Jack said, wiping the sweat from his forehead and making it even dirtier.

Cal raised an eyebrow. "That's what they all say."

He began heaving at the stubborn stake again.

"Why do you have this stupid stake in here anyways?" the old man asked.

"I don't even remember," Jack said. Grunting, he pushed and pulled the stake around and around to loosen it.

"All I know is that—" he paused, pulling with all his might. The stake suddenly broke loose, sending him off-balance and right onto his backside "—it's a pain in the rear," he finished.

Cal doubled over with laughter.

"So hilarious," Jack groaned as he sat in the dirt. "My tailbone is gonna be sore for days."

"Pain is just weakness leaving the body," the old man said, giving Jack a hand up. "At least, that's what your mom said when she gave birth to you."

Now they both doubled over laughing.

Wiping the tears from his eyes-which only smudged dirt all over his face-Jack grabbed the newly uprooted stake and started back toward the house.

For the first time in a long time, Jack started to feel hopeful. If a school teacher could take a fighter pilot's tales and calm a room of rowdy kids, maybe there was hope for him to get out of his mess.

The elder man put his hand on Jack's shoulder, and said, "Making Riley happy and content is your most important responsibility. She's your lifesaver, Jack. Don't neglect her."

Chapter 6: "If I Don't Take Responsibility, Nobody Will"

"BEEP! BEEP!"

Jack opened his eyes and shook his head, confused. He tried to make sense of where he was, what noise was blaring and why it was going on and on.

"BEEP! BEEP! BEEP!" it continued.

Then his head cleared and it all suddenly made sense again. His eyes focused on the bright red numbers on the clock: *6:31 am.*

Shocked, Jack leaped out from under his covers. He bounded over to the closet, grabbed a pair of work clothes and began pulling them on, hopping around the room like a freshman late for the first day of class.

Riley rolled over and looked at her husband running about.

"What's the big rush?" she moaned, squinting at the light floating in from their master bathroom.

"I'm late for work!" Jack responded impatiently, knowing deep down it was not her fault.

He reached for the bedroom doorknob, planning to head straight for the garage and skip breakfast. But as he swung the door open, he stopped.

"You have to start working fewer hours."

His mentor's words echoed from their conversation the previous week.

"Why are you still spending long hours processing all that paperwork, Jack?"

"I guess anyone can do it..." he had agreed.

But will anyone step up? Anyone can do it, but will they? he thought to himself.

"Take care of your wife... If you create an incredible business but destroy your family, you haven't succeeded at anything."

He looked back at his wife who had fallen asleep again.

"She's your lifesaver."

Jack quietly closed the door and cautiously made his way down the hall, realizing his commotion might wake up the entire house. He thought of his kids and how quickly they were growing up.

Suddenly, his perspective shifted.

How could I be so blind? he thought. *If I lose Riley and the kids what is my business worth?"*

He made his way down the stairs, walking like he had all day now. He stopped at the kitchen entry, thinking, considering, confused as to how to proceed with this change in perspective.

And then he knew and he immediately set to work. He did have all day. Work could wait, but his family wouldn't.

"Who am I helping if I can't even help them?" he whispered to no one.

Jack found he suddenly had new enthusiasm for the day. Flinging open the cupboard doors, he grabbed a pan and a spatula. He swiveled around on his heel and grabbed the last three slices of bacon from the fridge. He turned on the stove, laid the bacon in the frying pan, and listened for the sizzle.

He rushed—almost leaped—to the other side of the kitchen again and grabbed the coffee but stopped. It had been so long since he'd made coffee, he couldn't remember what ratios to use.

Just then he heard a stir from around the corner. He looked back to see his daughter Emma watching him, looking perplexed.

"Emma! You're just who I need!" he exclaimed. "How much coffee do I need to make two cups?"

"Just two cups?" she asked, even more perplexed.

"Like two mugs for two people! How much water and coffee do I need to make some for two people?"

"Well," she said, assuming a master's persona, "if you're going to make this much coffee"—she pointed at the 4-cup line on the pot—"you'll need this many scoops of grounds," she explained as she put 5 tablespoons of coffee grounds into the maker.

"That's how much Mom puts in. She says she doesn't like Grandma's coffee because it's always weak."

Jack smiled down at his intelligent daughter. What a gift she was.

"Thanks, hun," he said before a sizzling reminded him he had bacon on the stove. He rushed over to move it to the paper towels he had prepared.

"What's all this?" Riley's voice came floating through the entryway as she strolled, yawning, into the kitchen.

"Breakfast, can't you see?" Jack replied happily as he cracked an egg into the bacon lathered frying pan.

"Jack Martin making breakfast? Surely not," Riley joked, squinting a little.

Jack put his arm around his wife and kissed her. Emma rolled her eyes and left, groaning.

"I'm sorry for being caught up in my own little world," he said. "Cal has been helping me see how flawed my thinking has been. I can't keep going like this. I've got to slow down."

Riley looked up with admiration. She grinned as he talked.

"I really am sorry about all I've missed," he continued. "Jimmy's ball games, Emma's recitals-the church banquet. All the random times we could've spent together, but didn't 'cause I had my head in an engine," he said with a cocked eyebrow.

Jack's soul began to fill with a new enthusiasm for life and for his family. His heart overflowed with love for Riley. Yes, it felt right. This was the right track for him to follow.

"So, I thought making breakfast for the two of us was the least I could do to show my love and gratitude before work," he said, kissing her again.

"Jack," Riley said, looking into his eyes, with a grin.

"What?"

"It's Saturday."

JACK RAN across the park lawn, laughing along with his kids.

The sun shone warm in the late morning sky. The trees burst with a summer breeze that rustled the branches and sent loose leaves fluttering to the ground. Fall was approaching, which pleased the autumn loving mechanic, but it disappointed him that both of his kids would soon be going to school.

He looked over at his wife who sipped a latte on a nearby park bench. Beside her sat his old mentor. They were laughing as Jack goofed off with his delighted children. Though he was still troubled by the plateau he felt at his shop, his heart was full again.

Perhaps there was hope.

"It's good to see you haven't forgotten your fun side," his old friend bellowed as Jack approached, breathing heavily from all the running, "though you look a bit out of shape!" The man grinned broadly.

"I'd like to see *you* keep up with them!" Jack shot back, with a long sigh. They laughed.

Riley got up to take the children home.

"So, you decided to take me seriously, huh? Work less. Care for your family. Do things only you can do?"

"Yeah, I guess so. Thanks for talking straight to me," Jack said. "Hey, you up for a walk?"

"Why sure, if it's not too far. I'm an old man, ya know."

"There's a cafe just up the street."

"Well, then, by all means."

"I AM liking the idea of working less," Jack explained to Cal as they walked along. "But I have this gnawing fear that if I don't take responsibility for things, nobody else will."

Jack looked at his mentor beside him. The old man walked methodically, breathing slowly in and out like a trained athlete.

Jack wondered what wealth of wisdom and experience the man held untapped within that old gray frame.

"Many entrepreneurs feel the same way, Jack," Cal finally replied, "especially entrepreneurs of your type. You're not alone. Be encouraged."

Jack paused, waiting for the old man to continue, but he just kept walking and breathing.

The old man looked up and then over at Jack.

"What?" he asked, in reply to Jack's expectant gaze.

"I just thought you'd have a story about this or something."

"Oh, I suppose I do. But you don't want to be bored by that on a Saturday." Cal brushed it aside. "You only promised to give me two hours a week, remember?" He smiled broadly.

"I've got all day," Jack laughed.

"Well, then, I'll tell you about Charlie."

"AS YOU know, Charlie is a lifelong rancher," Cal began.

Jack nodded, remembering some of the rancher's recent projects mentioned over breakfast.

"The astounding thing about Charlie"—he drew each word out in his deep, radio bass—"is that by the time he turned everything over to his son, he didn't work much over 30 hours a week, if my memory serves me correctly. And it wasn't because he was lazy."

Jack stopped in his tracks and looked at his mentor, incredulous.

"He's a rancher! How could he do that?"

"Hold your horses, son!" the man said, holding up his hands before putting them behind his back and continuing his slow stroll. "That's the story I'm about to tell you."

He continued, "Charlie is the literal definition of a workhorse. He's like Kip, only more horse and less puppy. Has been ever since I first met him."

"Where did you meet him?" Jack inquired.

"Tucson. It was a Saturday morning. He was making a quick trip down just to deliver an old bull and a couple of heifers he had sold. That was Charlie. Always runnin' over time on the smallest things.

"I met him at a diner Kip had recommended. We soon discovered we were both visiting from Colorado, so we struck up a friendship.

"Amy and I once took him up on an invitation to visit his ranch. It was spring of '81, I believe, and the place was just splendid. I mean rugged, fresh, wild, beauty. We stayed in a little cottage they had up in the hills, couple hundred yards from the ranch house.

"Anyways, like I said, Charlie worked hard and took serious responsibility for his life, his home, and especially his ranch.

"This is obviously a great trait for a businessman and a leader—to take responsibility. But as they say, your greatest strength is often your greatest weakness. It was hard for

Charlie to keep employees for more than a year or two because he never developed them to their full potential."

"How do you mean?" Jack asked.

"Well, take for instance those three cows he brought down to Tucson when I met him."

"Yeah?"

"Charlie didn't have any other business down there. His only purpose was to sell those cows. An experienced ranch hand could've easily done that. Instead, the head rancher himself took time out of his busy schedule to travel over ten hours just to sell a few cows."

The men arrived at the cafe and sat down after they had ordered their drinks.

"Okay, so you're saying Charlie should have had a ranch hand take care of transporting the cattle?"

"Yes, but not just any hand. Someone he had trained for the job," the old man replied. "Obviously you don't just let any inexperienced joe take the cattle into their own hands. Obviously they need to be licensed to drive a truck. But even beyond that, Charlie should've—and he eventually learned this—taken one of his ranch hands aside and taught him how to transport livestock, interact with customers and buyers, and all that.

"Ownership." Jack's mentor growled the word out like an old time preacher. "As an employer—or as any type of leader—you want those under you to take ownership of their jobs. And that first and foremost begins with the leader."

"If a leader is always telling people what to do or, worse yet, doing it himself, they won't take ownership."

The old man paused as he took a sip of coffee.

"You want the floor sweeper to take *ownership* of the cleanliness of the floor. That floor is his. If he doesn't sweep it, nobody will. He should take pride in it.

"Or, on the ranch, you want a ranch hand to take ownership of his job, whether that's maintaining the place, transporting livestock, or wrangling horses. Let me give you another example from Charlie," the old man interrupted himself.

"So if a ranch uses horses to do work, they need what is called a wrangler, right?" Jack nodded, pretending to know. "This man is in charge—or should be—of all horse-related activities, which includes breeding and training-stuff like that.

"Well, in the early days of the ranch, Charlie hired a supposed 'wrangler' so he could tend to other, more important ranch oversight, business strategy, and whatnot.

"After a while, Charlie wanted the guy to start training one of their colts. So he says to him, 'Lenny, this horse has known you since birth. You have gained the necessary experience, now I want you to halter train it.'

"And so Charlie goes about his business for a couple days, even went on a trip out of state. When he came back, what do you know but the colt still wasn't trained. He found the thing wandering around and unapproachable in the yard with a halter and loose rope dangling from its neck.

"Boy, was Charlie unhappy. He stormed off in a sweat and searched the ranch high and low until he found the wrangler in the stable cleaning stalls. It was all Charlie could do to not wrangle the wrangler! In a mad huff, Charlie fired him on the spot."

"On the spot?" Jack asked.

"With no explanation! Not a word from the wrangler as to why he hadn't trained the colt or from Charlie as to why he fired the poor guy."

"Ouch. That's harsh."

"Sure was!" Swirling his coffee, Cal crossed his legs and leaned back in his chair. "After that, Charlie was a little gun-shy of negligent employees. If he was afraid something wasn't going to get done, instead of working with his employees and empowering them to take ownership, he just did it himself. Which is why he ran into a traveling man and his wife at a diner just outside of Tucson, Arizona." The old man pointed at himself so Jack would make the connection.

After draining his drink, Cal leaned forward, slapped the table and said, "Well, where shall we go now?"

Jack stifled a chuckle and exclaimed, "I thought you were old and didn't want to walk very far?"

"Well, whatever that ex-press-o stuff was you ordered for me has me roaring to go!" He slapped the table again and gave a hearty laugh.

"We can go back to the house or walk over to the shop, I suppose," Jack suggested.

"Where you lead, I will follow!"

"So, how did Charlie get his work week down to thirty hours?" Jack asked, as he stood from the table.

"Really, at the core he had to learn the same principles Kip did, which was to focus on doing what only he could. But there were different reasons behind why each of them was distracted with the little stuff.

"For Kip, his work was his drug, so he just did anything and everything, wasting away his energy and time for his family. Charlie, however, was simply afraid nothing would get done if he didn't make it happen. A bad experience skewed his perspective.

"On one hand, it is the employer's job to nurture an environment where employees take ownership. On the other hand, there are 'just-tell-me-what-to-do' employees out there who are too passive to take ownership. You have to weed those out during the hiring process. In any case, the responsibility does rest ultimately on the boss."

The old man slowed down, apparently remembering his age, despite the influx of caffeine. Jack grinned to himself. It felt good to do casual things with his old mentor again.

"By the time I really got to know Charlie, Kip had been meeting with Carl and me for several years already. So we invited Charlie to join us because we thought he would bring a lot to the table and figured we had a lot to offer him in return.

"As he shared about his business and the barriers he kept coming up against, it became obvious to us that he had become an obsessive micromanager. Because Kip had a similar experience, he spoke directly into Charlie's situation and lifestyle, pointing out how he had to loosen his grip on the ranch and let his employees take ownership—like we've been talking about.

"Not surprisingly, the first two moves he made were to hire and train a self-motivated and creative wrangler, as well as a driver who could transport livestock and execute business deals. Those two things in themselves relieved a lot of stress and time off his shoulders. This freed him to work on moving the ranch forward, exploring new ventures with breeding and feeding and whatever other things ranchers do to innovate when they finally have time."

Cal smiled as he concluded the story.

"So, '*Do what only you can do*,' again," Jack summarized, "and '*empower ownership*.'"

"Exactly right," Cal agreed. "If you execute those two concepts, your productivity will drastically increase."

Chapter 7: Unmasking the Facade

CARS WHIZZED past as Jack made his way from the cafe on Lewis Street. He shoved his hands deeper into his pockets to escape the crisp morning air. The cold always energized him and he whistled as he mulled over his recent conversations with his mentor.

He was beginning to see the value of a Winning Circle or "doing business in strong community," as Cal put it. It bothered Jack how many misconceptions he had blindly believed about business! So much for four years of personal experience.

Jack fiddled with the coins in his pocket, trying to keep his hands out of the breeze. The expense of joining a Winning Circle didn't bother him now. If the success of these men was due at all to the support and feedback of the group, he wanted it too, even if it cost him.

His only hang-up was the sharing. No matter how much sense it made, the idea of sharing his deepest struggles with peers still made him uncomfortable. Talking to his mentor, putting his family first—he was getting used to all of that. But sharing openly with other men his age seemed humiliating.

He stopped at the edge of the sidewalk and pushed the button for the crosswalk.

"Hey Jack, good mornin'!" a voice called from behind him. He recognized Charlie's western twang immediately. "You meet with Cal again after breakfast?" he asked, strolling up beside Jack.

"Yeah I did," Jack said. "I never realized how much experience he has. He's learned a lot through you guys."

"He's a wise man. How's it going for ya?" Charlie asked.

"Good!" Jack replied.

Charlie grinned down at the younger man, arms on his hips as if waiting expectantly for something more.

Jack returned Charlie's gaze hesitantly, unsure how to handle the silence.

"Good?" Charlie repeated. "In what way?"

Jack fumbled for the words. "Well, like I said, I've learned a lot." He felt the butterflies in his stomach begin their less-than-synchronized flying.

Charlie kept grinning. "How are things going, really?"

Jack could feel his palms start to sweat. His heartbeat quickened. He felt his face turn red and hoped the rancher hadn't seen the embarrassment wash over him.

The pressure increased in his chest, twisting his stomach into knots, until finally it all bubbled over and came tumbling out in a rush of words and sweat and red cheeks.

Jack felt like a fifth grader spilling his silly secrets to the teacher.

He explained the emotions he had pent up inside him. How every Friday morning he felt like a kid at the adult table.

He told Charlie how it was embarrassing simply to share his struggles even with a kind, trusted old mentor. He couldn't imagine what it would be like to share with his peers.

"I've racked up substantial debt that I'm *still* trying to pay off. And even after four years, I still feel lost in leading my small team!" he vented. "I'm just a mechanic, Charlie. I'm totally out of place among men running companies in industries far more important and demanding than an auto-repair shop." He sputtered the words as if in disdain. "I feel like-I feel like a little boy lost..."

He trailed off, realizing he had rambled for several minutes and looked sheepishly at the older man. But Charlie didn't laugh. He didn't scold. He didn't even look at his phone or fidget restlessly. He listened. He looked right into Jack's eyes, nodding and smiling occasionally. Jack stood there uncomfortably folding and unfolding his arms.

"I guess I just feel like a naive schoolboy among them—you," Jack concluded.

Taking his hat off and motioning for Jack to follow him, Charlie sat down on the curb. Jack felt a little conspicuous but followed the rancher's lead and sat. He was shivering now. He noticed the crosswalk sign had turned red again.

Charlie stretched out his long legs into the street and smiled at Jack. "I love mornings like this," he said, closing his eyes and letting the sun warm his face. Jack shivered.

"You know what," Charlie began, eyes still closed, "I felt the exact same way you do when I first started meetin' with the group." He shoved his thumb in the direction of the cafe behind them.

"Really?" Jack asked. "How so?"

"Well, imagine it. There I was, this rough 'n' tumble, boots and hat wearing cowboy. And there they were, a successful multi-restaurant owner, a pilot, and, eventually, an educated teacher. Carl understands rough 'n' tumble, being in the Air Force and all, but even he has been refined and educated into a professional pilot." He spread his long arms out into a shrug. "What did I know about their businesses? And of all things, why would they care about my lowly ranch? But," he said, "I found—and I'm sure you have, too—that they really don't care if we fit their style or not."

He paused, turning his hat around in his hands. "When I started sharing with the others about embarrassing obstacles or revenue losses on the ranch, they continued to respect me. They didn't treat me as less valuable to the group. I realized for the first time I possessed worth simply because I was a livin', breathin' human individual. It wasn't because I was turning a large profit or because I was a dynamic leader—but simply because I lived and breathed."

He absentmindedly shoved some gravel into the street with his leather boots.

"You know," he said, "successful people can be the warmest and most welcoming people around. You know why I think that is?" He looked at Jack.

"Why?"

"Because almost all of them have been in our shoes. They are 'failures'"—he lifted his fingers in quotes—"just like us. But they got back up, they pushed on, they sat at tables they didn't belong at. Those crazy successful people are some of the most flawed, but it's their flaws that helped them succeed. It's okay not to be perfect and not have all the answers. Just learn from it and get back up again."

Jack shifted his weight as he sat, watching the crosswalk sign turn green for the third time.

"That makes sense," he told the old rancher, sighing.

"*Hhhuhh!*" Charlie imitated Jack's sigh. "What's '*hhhuhh!*' about?"

"Oh, I guess I still fear I'll never be able to grow my business or pay down my debt."

Charlie thought about it, then said, "I worried about that too, which is why it was so good for me to be in this group and share my struggles. I talked constantly about my financial frustrations and how hard it was to turn a profit on a ranch. But eventually they helped me to let go of the need to generate results and focus on things that really mattered."

Jack looked confused.

"Exactly!" Charlie agreed. "I had the same reaction. But I discovered the more desperate I got to turn a profit the more frustrated my employees and I were. Eventually, I learned to focus only on building healthy systems with my team, my finances, and my relationships. With healthy systems in place results come—slowly, but eventually and with stability.

"It's like this," he said, "I don't do much with crops myself, but business is kind of like a farmer who plants a seed into the ground. He puts in place systems to plant, water, and tend the seed until harvest. Sometimes business is just a matter of plantin' and waterin' seeds, and waitin' for them to grow. But that takes patience and a willin'ness to forgo short-term success for long-term sustainability and easy management."

"So you did that on your ranch?" Jack asked. "You let go of the drive to turn a profit and instead set up systems?"

"Yeah, because you can work on systems and maintain them over the long haul—they're sustainable. Whereas when you're just runnin' around doing business by the seat of your pants tryin' to make an immediate profit, you will eventually burn out your engine, as it were."

"So, just like that you changed?" Jack asked.

"Well, it wasn't on a dime. It was a slow process of learnin' from the others and failin'—which proved to me they were right," he said, waving his arm in the direction of the cafe again. "But learnin' and failin' wasn't the worst of it. As I began to see the light, I had to do one of the hardest things I've ever done."

"What was that?"

"I had to ask people close to me—these gentlemen as well as relatives—to lend me some money to get through the year—this was about six months after I joined them. The scariest part was I had no idea how I was goin' to pay them back." The rancher shook his head. "I don't recommend it as a business strategy, but it's where I was at. It was hard asking for help"—he scrunched up his nose—"but you know what?"

"What?"

"When I expressed my need for help," he said, "I got tremendous support from everyone. They rallied right around me and helped me through. That's the power of doing business within strong community."

"'Business within strong community,'" Jack repeated. "Cal says that."

"You said you were embarrassed to share your struggles just now," the rancher asked.

"Yeah, kind of," Jack said.

"Did I make you feel stupid?"

Jack shook his head.

"Did I walk away from you?"

"No. You were very encouraging, why?"

"As you were talking and unloading everything you had kept inside for so long, did you feel better?"

"Yeah, I guess," Jack shrugged.

"I bet," the rancher said, holding up a finger, "you even begin to see solutions for some of your problems just through talking about them, am I right?"

"Well," Jack stammered, "I don't know if they're solutions."

"That's what can happen when you and others share and brainstorm together!" Charlie smiled at the younger man. "Jack, you know good men. I know you do because you are a good man and good men attract good friends. Go, find them and start sharin'. Start, as Carl says, 'a lifestyle of contribution.' Start your own Winning Circle, Jack."

The younger man mumbled a reply, trying to think it through.

"Well, the day's leavin' us behind!" Charlie declared as he stood up. He pointed at the pedestrian sign "Light's green now."

CHARLIE LEFT Jack alone to his thoughts.

The mechanic was thinking of all the businessmen and leaders who he could invite to his own Winning Circle. It still felt weird to him, imagining how the conversation would go.

"Hey, you wanna get together and talk about our problems?" Jack would ask.

The friend would probably wrinkle his nose and shake his head. *"I'm sorry, Jack, I have important things to do."*

Jack blushed just thinking about it.

He slowly rose from the curb and watched Charlie stroll away humming to himself. Jack tried to imagine what the rancher must have been like in his younger years.

Probably wore the same jean outfit. He chuckled to himself.

The light turned green again and Jack crossed the street, climbed into his truck, and went to work.

JACK HAD begun to view his shop from a new perspective. He no longer felt intense pressure to make something of himself. Yet he also took comfort in knowing success was possible.

Stepping inside the dusty office, he paused. He looked at the piles of bills, flyers, and *Popular Mechanics* magazines strewn across the desk over his laptop.

A thought occurred to him and instantly he knew what to do. Leaning out the office door, Jack shouted to the young men in the shop.

"Hey, Gabriel!" he called. "Come here for a sec'!"

The 18-year-old looked at his co-workers nervously before jogging toward the office.

"Yeah, boss?" he said.

"Do you enjoy working here, Gabe?"

"Yes sir, I appreciate the job!" he said, a little too enthusiastically to be genuine.

"You like changing oil and grabbing tools and parts for me and Pete?"

"Happy to help wherever I can, sir," the young man assured.

"But aren't you good with computers? Wouldn't you rather be somewhere else messing around with computers and software and stuff?" Jack asked.

"I mean, I suppose so. But I didn't get a job like that. You hired me and I'm glad to be working."

"Would you enjoy doing the computer work for the shop?" Jack asked the teenager.

Gabe thought for a second. "I've never really considered it. I suppose I could enjoy it."

"You'd enjoy it more than working on the cars, I bet?" Jack said, perceiving restraint in the answer.

"Actually, to be honest, sir, yes, I would," the young man admitted.

"It's all yours then," Jack said. "If you want it, I'll give you responsibility over all the computer work: records, scheduling, billing—all of that.'"

Gabe put his hand over his chin, as if considering the negotiation.

"I'll bump up your pay to be worth it. If you agree, all of this"—he spread his hands out to the office—"will be your domain."

"All of it?" Gabe exclaimed.

"Yup! I'll move my stuff over there," Jack said, motioning to the desk in the corner, hidden by boxes, papers, and parts. "And you can do whatever you need to be comfortable with this desk."

He thought a little more, eyeing the rest of the office.

"Perhaps I'll bring my wife in and get her to help shine this place up and make it a little more pleasant and welcoming. Otherwise, it's all yours. Are you cool with this? Do you want to give it a try for a while and reevaluate later?"

"Yes, sir—I mean no, sir—I mean I want to do it."

"Good! You ready to start?"

"Yes, sir!"

"Okay, I'll go over everything with you as soon as I clear away this junk."

Jack started looking through all the stuff on his desk. He stacked the magazines together and tossed them into the trash. Setting all the bills and business paperwork right next to the computer, he began sorting through the loose-leaf papers. A little flyer caught his attention:

"Share, learn, and grow with people like you!" it read. "Join us at our weekly business breakfast!"

JACK COULDN'T believe what he was doing. Upon finding the invitation, he had called the number and asked to visit the next Saturday.

Now he sat around a restaurant table with five other businessmen, four of whom he had never met before, and one who was none other than Mr. Robertson, the roofer. Jack laughed at himself as he remembered the half-hearted conversation he'd had with the roofer at the church banquet. His perspective had changed dramatically since then.

They were going around the table sharing about themselves so Jack could get to know them better. It all reminded him of the group of retired men who met every Friday morning in the cafe on Lewis Street. Only these guys were his own age.

Each one talked about their businesses, why they had started, what they had gone through and overcome, and what they hoped would happen in the future.

Then it was Jack's turn. His heart beat a little faster. Adrenaline surged through his body. His lip quivered a little as he spoke.

"I ... it ... it," he stuttered and blushed, but he pushed through. "To be honest, it freaks me out to share my problems with you."

There. He had it out. The men chuckled.

"Believe me, we've all been there, bro," the leader, a guy named Kyle, assured Jack. "Just say whatever you're comfortable sharing."

Jack continued, explaining some of his backstory and the current state of his business. The more he shared the easier it got. He even told them some of the humiliating details, such as his debt, and how long it had taken him to realize his wife should be a top priority over his business.

"It's hard—and embarrassing—for me to share this. In fact, it has taken me a long time to even see the value of a group like this," he told the men.

Their continual nodding and expressions of agreement relieved Jack. They seemed to understand what he was talking about.

Charlie had been right. It felt good to share with people who understood and still respected him. Plus, they had good insight into some of his problems, even though none of them were mechanics.

Jack knew he would be joining them the next week and every week after that. These guys were real men, successful, strong, brilliant. Yet they spoke freely about their weaknesses. They even asked him—the new guy—for input, which he shared humbly. Being able to contribute to other people's success boosted his own confidence and motivation to work hard towards success himself.

Jack sat back and smiled. His old friend would be delighted; he had found his "strong community".

Chapter 8: Not Just Shooting the Breeze

Three Years Later...

THE OWNER of Jack's Auto-Repair drove his old Tacoma into the garage for the last time.

Pete, the newest chief mechanic in town, waved at his boss.

"Good mornin'!" he greeted the smiling Jack.

"Morning!" the boss replied. "You ready for this?"

"Yes sir!"

Jack's eight-year-old son Jimmy jumped out of the truck and ran into the office.

The mechanic had done himself proud over the previous three years. Customers bragged freely about their favorite mechanic shop and how well they treated their customers.

"That garage on Main. It's the best. If they can't getcha in right away, they'll make you a priority later on. That young secretary of theirs, he'll even call you up personally to tell you when there's a new opening available. Can't beat their prices or efficiency either!"

Jack Martin walked into his old office. Jimmy hung off Gabe as the poor secretary tried to continue working on the computer.

"Careful, Jimmy. You bother Gabe too much and he might not want you to come back!" Jack joked.

He stood still, taking it all in. The place was in tip-top shape. Riley had done herself proud in decorating the office so anyone would feel comfortable waiting in it. Apart from the dead flowers on the coffee table, it was just how she had arranged it.

But the time had come for Jack to move on. He loved the thrill of presenting people with restored vehicles but he realized he loved helping restore lives even more. He had done what he could to transform lives through the shop. He was proud of what he had done there. Pete had superseded even Jack in skill, Nate had moved on with a bigger, better company, and Gabe was working his way through college while using computers to renovate the entire environment at the repair shop.

Jack gathered what was left on his desk into his briefcase. With one last thank you and handshake, he said goodbye and drove away.

But there was still one last thing to do before he left town.

"WHAT DID he say?"

Jack and his mentor were back at their regular spot after Friday morning breakfast.

"He thought all we did at the meetings was shoot the breeze. He was like, 'I've got a few friends I play golf with on the weekends. Isn't that the same thing?'"

They chuckled at the thought.

"What did you say then?"

"I told him it's much more than that," Jack said. "We do spend time catching up, but we're intentional about helping each other grow."

"Some people are so skeptical at first, aren't they?" Cal winked.

Jack chuckled and rolled his eyes.

"I think you said it right. Every Winning Circle should take time to make small-talk and catch up. Good camaraderie is important for deep growth to happen. But at the same time, we don't want to waste their valuable time. The discussions should be focused on things that matter."

"How did you guys do it?"

Cal mused. "We made a lot of mistakes along the way, as I'm sure your group does too," he explained. "But we learned quickly it was easy to make false assumptions. Once we figured this out, we began taking time to ask clarifying questions whenever someone shared a story or problem before we assumed we knew the answer."

"Makes sense," Jack agreed.

"Everyone comes at life and business from different angles—which is the beauty of the Winning Circle. But our differences can cause misunderstandings, which easily result in wrong assumptions. We made sure we clearly understood each situation. Remember, just because your perspective is different doesn't mean you're right *nor* does it mean you're wrong. It just means you're different. So don't hesitate to share your perspective, it will be very helpful. But also never assume you know the right or wrong answer."

Jack loved listening to his old mentor, especially when he got passionate. Even after years of learning from him, Jack knew he still had a storehouse of untapped wisdom.

"Also, something else we found helpful was to pick one thing to act on every week. There are a hundred suggestions you could try to implement every week. You just can't. So, after brainstorming together, we chose one thing each of us would do that week. And we made it a priority because nothing ever changes if you don't prioritize it. Make it as important as eating. But don't try to do everything at once."

"How do you make it a priority?"

"Well, depending on what type of assignment it was, I literally made it as important as eating. If I was trying to develop a daily habit, I would refuse to eat lunch until I had done it."

Jack was already thinking of the chicken sandwich he was going to have for lunch. His stomach growled. "What else did you do?"

The old mentor thought for a moment.

"Ah!" he finally said. "Here's a neat trick we learned several years after doing the same thing over and over again. Structure is important, but we found it sometimes gets really monotonous. When this happens, people easily disengage from the group. So we took time to change things up. For example, sometimes we each shared from books we had recently read, sometimes going so far as to rent a facility and actually teaching it to each other. Other times, we'd all attend a seminar together. This was especially fun if it was out of state because it meant we could take a road trip. Sometimes we'd go just as guys, other times we'd bring our wives and make a grand party out of it."

Jack wondered what it would be like to road trip with these passionate men.

"So where did the structure come from?" Jack asked.

"You know how Charlie likes to talk a lot?" Cal asked Jack, eyes twinkling.

"Yes, sir!" Jack chuckled.

Cal laughed. "Well, if you think he talks a lot now, you should have seen him when he first came. He wouldn't be seated at the table two minutes before he'd have us all wrapped up in some grand story." Cal smiled as he spoke. "As much as we loved Charlie and his stories, we knew that's not why any of us were attending the meeting. This taught us two things. Number one, we needed an official moderator; Carl was the obvious choice, since he already did it informally. Number two, we needed to set boundaries.

"As you know, the meetings originally were born out of our note-swapping in college. After Carl and I finished the class and still wanted to keep sharing ideas back and forth, we started meeting at a cafe not too far from campus. "When it was just the two of us, things went pretty smoothly and naturally. But soon Kip started coming and then Charlie and Trev.

"We hashed things out so hard! We'd tear each idea apart and brainstorm how to put it back together—it was great!" The old man laughed again. "But we all felt—especially at the behest of Carl—like we could get more done if we were more intentional with our time.

"So with Carl at the helm, we structured our meetings. That's when we came up with what you saw every week—or pretty close to it at least. Obviously it has evolved over the years, especially after we all retired."

"How'd you come up with the 'hot-seat'?" Jack asked.

"It just kind of evolved, as I recall. It likely started when Carl and I first went up to visit Kip. We saw how helpful it was for him to just share freely without interruption. The input we gave was good too, I'm sure. But the magic was in the sharing. Soon we were all doing it. From there, we naturally started brainstorming each problem together. And every week we'd follow-up."

Jack's mentor leaned back and crossed his legs.

"Once, we invited a guy named Adam to join us. He was a construction worker or something along those lines, I don't remember. He came for several weeks before we all convinced Carl to ask him to leave."

Jack gasped. "I never knew this! Why on earth?" he asked.

"Because he was all talk, talk, talk and no action. He'd sit in the 'hot-seat' and share all his problems week after week. But we quickly realized he kept having the same problems, which would've been fine if the guy had honestly tried our advice. But it became obvious he wasn't taking it seriously. We felt like he was taking advantage of the group and stealing our time. So we asked him to leave."

Jack raised his eyebrows. "Ouch," he said.

"Yeah, it wasn't fun for either him or us. We all felt bad. But we valued our time and the integrity of the group. That's when we started choosing weekly 'assignments' after every session and being more careful who we allowed to join us."

"Wow, you guys were serious," Jack said.

The conversation lulled and they sipped their coffee in silence.

"So, uh," Cal finally said, "you're all packed?"

"Yup," Jack replied.

"This old town's not gonna be the same without ya, son." Jack thought he saw a tear slipping down his old mentor's face.

"Yeah, we're going to miss it."

"Don't forget about me, now. Visit at least once a year."

The old man smiled, unashamed at the tears now streaming down his face.

"Only if you do the same!" Jack said. "Thanks for everything, Cal."

"I wouldn't have it any other way. I'm so proud of you, Jack Martin."

Epilogue

THE OLD man watched his friend walk out of the cafe. He turned a small paper over in his hands and considered it before stuffing it back inside his pocket. It could wait.

Jack had come a long ways since his traumatic childhood. In many ways he had already surpassed Cal as a leader and team-builder. But some doors in Jack's heart-long locked and shut off to the world-had not yet been opened and freed. Deep in Jack's soul, a little boy still wandered in the woods, alone, broken, and confused.

"MISTER! HELP me!" the little boy cried to the stranger. "My arm really hurts!"

"What are you doing here, son?" the man asked little Jack. "Where are your parents?'

"I-I don't know," Jack replied. "I was playing in the woods and running, when I slipped and hurt my arm. Now I'm lost."

"What are your parents names?"

"Maa-mma..." the boy trailed off. "I don't know," he said.

"What's your name?"

"Jack Martin," the boy replied confidently. "I'm six years old."

"Jack Martin. What a nice name," the man said warmly. "It's not always good for little boys to talk to strangers, but since you can't find your home, I'll take you to mine. I'll fix you a nice hot cup of cocoa while we wait for the Sheriff."

"Thank you, Mister-mister..."

"Please, call me Cal."

Acknowledgments

Let's face it. I could never have written this book alone.

Christopher Witmer, thank you for the long hours you spent crafting the plot and hunting for the correct "turn of the phrase". You took my ideas and brought them to life with your love for storytelling and communication.

Heidi Coblentz, thank you for poring over the manuscript. Not only did you catch countless typos and grammatical errors, but you also uncovered significant inconsistencies in the storyline. Your watchful eye brought much-needed cohesion to the book.

Thank you!

www.ingramcontent.com/pod-product-compliance
Lightning Source LLC
Chambersburg PA
CBHW060615210326
41520CB00010B/1345